PORTFOLIO
BEING ETHICAL

Professor S. Manikutty has specialized in business policy and strategy, and his areas of interest include strategic management and competitive strategy, leadership, global competitiveness of industries, corporate governance and strategies for family businesses. He is the regional editor of the *European Journal of International Management*; a member of the editorial boards of *Vikalpa*, published by IIM Ahmedabad, *Journal of Human Values*, published by IIM Calcutta, and *International Journal of Innovation and Incubation*, published by Chinese Business Incubation Association, Taiwan. He is also the associate editor of the *Journal of Asia Entrepreneurship and Sustainability*, which is published by St Paul University, Quezon City, Philippines.

INDIA'S BESTSELLING BUSINESS BOOKS SERIES

IIM

AHMEDABAD
BUSINESS BOOKS

BEING ETHICAL

Ethics as the Foundation of Business

S. MANIKUTTY

PORTFOLIO
PENGUIN

An imprint of Penguin Random House

PORTFOLIO

USA | Canada | UK | Ireland | Australia
New Zealand | India | South Africa | China | Singapore

Portfolio is part of the Penguin Random House group of companies
whose addresses can be found at global.penguinrandomhouse.com

Published by Penguin Random House India Pvt. Ltd
4th Floor, Capital Tower 1, MG Road,
Gurugram 122 002, Haryana, India

Penguin
Random House
India

First published in Random Business by Random House India 2011
Published by Penguin Random House India 2016
Published in Portfolio by Penguin Random House India 2018

15 14 13 12 11 10

The views and opinions expressed in this book are the author's own and the
facts are as reported by him which have been verified to the extent possible,
and the publishers are not in any way liable for the same.

ISBN 9788184001389

Printed at Manipal Technologies Limited, India

www.penguin.co.in

MIX
Paper | Supporting
responsible forestry
FSC® C043100

This is a legitimate digitally printed version of the book and therefore might not
have certain extra finishing on the cover.

To

Geetha

CONTENTS

CONTENTS

Introduction

The recent scandals in the world of business as, for instance, with Enron, WorldCom, Global Crossing, and Satyam have kindled a debate on the subject of business ethics. Management journals carry papers, commentaries, and discussions on business ethics, ethics in business, personal ethics of businessmen and managers, and so on. Invariably, some blame is laid at the door of business schools, as if business fraud was their invention; management thinkers and scholars indulge in considerable introspection (something they are particularly good at) and wonder, individually and collectively, whether they indeed had something to do with the state of affairs, and whether they can do something about it. Not many, of course, remember the great frauds in the UK and the USA, especially in the Antebellum Era, which made billionaires who later went on to become great philanthropists, much before the advent of formal management education. On a positive note, books on business ethics, with different approaches such as philosophical, conceptual case studies and plain old pontification, seem to be flourishing. Many adopt a position today that businesses are not solely for earning profits and for enhancing shareholder value; they should use ethics as *one of their foundations* for doing business. This is the position taken by this book: every manager has the obligation to ensure that the business is run not only on commercially sound lines but also on ethically sound lines, and an ethical organization should not be seen as an object of curiosity.

I wonder whether, in embarking on writing this book on business ethics, I need to confront a fundamental problem. If a manager is ethical, this book is not needed. If, on the other hand, he is not, then this book will not do any good anyway. How, then, could such a book be justified?

I believe that few managers are completely ethical or unethical. Most (happily) strive to be ethical, but struggle to find what that ethical solution is. This book is intended for this vast majority who confront ethical dilemmas, grapple with the issues, and seek a better understanding on the ethical issues involved in business as well as in personal life.

Another problem I confront is regarding what approach this book should take. This book is not for the philosopher who wishes to delve into the intricacies of ethical questions; it is meant for the working manager who perhaps wishes to know how he can build a more ethical organization and be more ethical at a personal level. Should I present the issues as a quick-fix guide, a sort of do-it-yourself book, or as a manual of ethics-in-six-easy-steps? A book on the legal aspects of business can summarize and tell the reader what those legal aspects are; a book on strategy can present a step-by-step approach on how to formulate strategy. But I believe that ethics is different; it is not possible to reduce ethics to a set of basic commandments and present them as a this-is-what-you-should-do module. One can, of course, devise a questionnaire, which will enable the reader to get a score on his ethical orientation and create an illusion of self-discovery; one could provide a step-by-step flow chart he could navigate through and arrive at what the ethical decisions are in a circumstance, creating an illusion of mastery of technique. But I believe that these are basically Sunday-

School approaches which are got over by Monday, and most of the recipients of these pieces would have eschewed them.

The trouble about ethical problems that managers confront in real life is that they are in the nature of dilemmas, and rarely have a clear-cut solution. There are few invariant imperatives that can be applied in all situations. What is right and ethical depends so much on the situation, on the actors involved, and on your own values that generalizations seem to be difficult. There can be no 'the best' or 'the right' solutions; there can only be a 'what is the best or right under the circumstances' solution. The worst thing is, the solutions cannot be found in a book; you have to figure them out yourself.

Why, then, this book? Because, even though there may not be any 'solutions' and 'answers' to ethical problems, managers should be aware of what questions to ask, what roadmap of questioning may lead to better resolution of the issues. Even though *the* answer may not exist, there may be *better* answers, which are worth seeking. Ethical issues are, in general, complex, and understanding this complexity itself may be a useful first step in arriving at better solutions.

ABOUT THIS BOOK

This book does not, therefore, adopt a 'step-by-step-guide-to-ethics' approach to arrive at *the* solutions; what it seeks to do is to take up the different dimensions in business ethics and explore and present the issues that arise. Thus there are ethical issues in dealing with customers, employees, competitors, the community, and the larger society. In each, there are a number of situations that pose different issues, which are complex and need to be understood. There are multiple points of view that need to be looked at and a common theme is that they all involve not solutions, but tradeoffs. Managers are to arrive at what seems to them to be the best tradeoffs.

Thus the book looks at ethical *dilemmas* rather than ethical *problems with a solution*. There are, of course, certain actions that are clearly unethical, and these are highlighted. But the more important value the book seeks to bring to you is to present you the picture in all its complexity, leaving you to figure out for yourself what you would do under the different situations presented.

TO WHOM THIS BOOK IS ADDRESSED

If you are one of those who feel that business and ethics do not mix, or believe that this is a practical world, and you do not get around by being ethical but by being smart, this book is not for you. If, on the other hand, you are one of those who believe that these two *can* go together, who are trying to run a business on ethical lines, and wish to imbue an ethical culture in your organization, then go on, read this book. I recognize your difficulties in being ethical or even defining what being ethical is, but am hopeful that you can improve the ethical climate of your organization, not necessarily perfectly, but at least by taking some steps in the right direction. As in personal life, it is up to you to decide where you want to be regarding ethics and chalk out a path to reach there.

LEGALITY AND ETHICS

You need to understand clearly at the outset the important distinction between legality and ethics. I highlight this point early because these are often confused; many managers think they are being ethical when all they are doing is simply making sure that their actions are legal. An action is legal (or not illegal) if it is in accordance with the provisions of law. This does not necessarily mean it is ethical. Managers necessarily have to act legally, but this only means their actions cannot be challenged in a court of law; it does not follow that the actions are ethical or morally right. Thus an insurance company denying a claim on some technical ground (for example, non-disclosure of an existing condition which may have nothing to do with the claim) or a product company setting out such conditions that make it virtually impossible to enforce a warranty on a product may be acting legally but not, perhaps, ethically. Conversely, certain actions can be illegal yet ethical, because they serve a larger societal interest. For example, using a phone tap to nab a criminal without proper approval may be illegal but may be ethical because it serves a larger purpose.

This book is not about the legal aspects of business; it does not tell you how to win cases in a court of law. Rather, it concerns the ethical aspects; it tells you how to be fair, just, and ethical in your dealings; how to judge the right/wrong of an action; what dimensions are to be considered; and how to take a holistic view of a complex problem.

THE MODE OF PRESENTATION IN THE BOOK

I have adopted what I hope is an easy-to-read style, shorn of jargon and deep philosophical discussion. In the field of ethics, some digression into philosophy is inevitable, but this is kept at an as easy-to-understand level as possible. In most of the chapters, there are brief illustrative examples (put in boxes) to enable you to relate the issues discussed to real-life situations. In each chapter, there are short insertions on 'What should an ethical manager do?', serving as sort of brief, quick-to-use guidelines that emerge after a discussion, although these should not be seen as quick fixes that I have cautioned you at the beginning to avoid. Finally, at the end of each chapter, the key takeaways are given as bullet points by way of a summary, with the caveat that they are mostly oversimplifications.

It is hoped that as you progress through the book, you would develop a framework for analysis of ethical issues that is your own, that is in congruence with your own value system, and, while taking an action, you are better aware of its ethical dimensions, and are aware of why you are taking that action.

Welcome to this messy territory. Watch your step!

1

Business Ethics? What is That?

'In making judgements, early kings were perfect, because they made moral principles the starting point of everything and the root of everything that was beneficial. This principle is, however, something people of mediocre intelligence never grasp. Not grasping it, they lack awareness, and lacking awareness, they just pursue profit. But while pursuing profit, it is absolutely impossible for them to be certain of attaining it.'

—Lü Bu-Wei, Chinese Prime Minister, 246 BC

Business organizations are an essential part of life today. You cannot live a moment without in some way coming in contact with business organizations, their products, managers, and their actions, and so on. It is because of their pervasive effects on everyone's lives that business organizations have been subject to intense study in their different aspects.

A corporation is a peculiar creature. It is a 'legal person': it can sue, it can be sued, it can enter into contracts, appoint and dismiss people, and so on. But can it commit ethical or unethical acts? Is there something called ethics of a particular *corporation* as distinct from ethics of the individuals, especially the top management, constituting it? Can you say that an action of a corporation is moral or immoral in the sense you can say that about individuals?

If you say corporations are 'morally responsible' for their acts, just what does it mean?

When you judge people's actions as moral or immoral, you are, consciously or unconsciously, employing some criteria for arriving at such judgements. Why cannot you then judge corporate actions by similar criteria? Or, can you?

If you find the actions of individuals as immoral, then those individuals can be punished by imposing fines on them, sending them to jail, or even executing them (as is indeed done in China). Can corporations be punished the same way individuals can be (of course, corporations cannot go to jail or be executed!)? If they can commit crimes but cannot be punished, what are the implications?

These issues are valid and important. But mere debate is not enough; increasingly, concerns are raised about the way corporate managers behave, whether in their individual capacities or in their 'managerial' or 'official' capacities. Ultimately, corporations are controlled by individuals and these individuals are the primary bearers of responsibility. Hence it is becoming more difficult to escape under the 'I did it for the corporation' excuse. When individuals take ethical positions, companies behave more responsibly; conversely, deterrent punishments to individuals can shape corporations' ways of doing business.

For many readers, the very phrase 'business ethics' may sound like an oxymoron. Can you conduct business on strictly ethical terms? Are business and ethics separate, and does business need to be ethically neutral, not unethical, but non-ethical, so to speak? With so much talk about corporate social responsibility, what exactly is this social responsibility? Is it for business to be socially responsible and, indeed, is it *ethically right* to be socially responsible? Milton Friedman, Nobel laureate in Economics from Chicago, once famously declared that 'the only social responsibility of business is to make profits' (1970). He argued that managers of a business are merely agents of the real 'owners' of the enterprise, who are its shareholders, and the managers of a corporation have only one mandate, namely, to maximize profits on behalf of the shareholders of the corporation. He, of course, added that this has to be done *legally*, that is, respecting the laws of the countries they work in, at least to the extent needed to keep them out of jail. There is no advice regarding their need to be *ethical*; indeed if being ethical leads to a reduction in shareholder value, the duty of the managers is clear: to opt for shareholder value. Deviation from this norm implies that the managers are compromising their fiduciary duty to their shareholders. This leads to a paradoxical formulation: Being ethical in business, if it leads to reduction in shareholder value, is unethical!

Friedman's view is a rather extreme one, and is by no means universally accepted. Many, including highly successful managers, feel that such a formulation is narrow, misleading, and dangerous. First, shareholders are only *one* of the groups of stakeholders, and not the only one. A manager's duty is towards multiple stakeholders, such as the company's employees, creditors, suppliers, customers, and the community it serves. Shareholders contribute just their capital, which is only *one* of the factors of production. Shareholders in fact have the *least* stake in the enterprise because they can always exit the firm by simply selling their shares, while the others do not have such an easy exit option, and sometimes no exit option at all. Second, it is by no means clear that the shareholders mandate the managers to resort to *any* (though legal) means to enhance their shareholder value. Thus the assumption of the mandate being to maximize shareholder value at any cost is just that: an assumption. Last, shareholders may want their *long-term* value to be maximized, and being ethical may lead to better performance and indeed survival of the firm in the long run. Hence managers do not serve shareholders if they achieve a short-run improvement in their shareholder value through unethical means.

Thus there *is* something called business ethics, and it is the purpose of this book to introduce you to the notion of business ethics, the issues involved, and the dilemmas in trying to manage ethically. Business ethics have many dimensions, and these are interlinked. The succeeding chapters examine each of these dimensions, their linkages, and the dilemmas involved in each. For, as is argued below, being ethical is not a simple choice of doing the right thing versus the wrong thing; it is to find a balance between multiple right and wrong choices, arriving at not a solution but a compromise. The book sees ethics as not just an optional extra, but as the *foundation* for running a business in the long run, and examines the problems and challenges in doing so.

ETHICS AS A FIELD OF ENQUIRY

Ethics is the enquiry into what is good. Ancient philosophers, especially the Greek, grappled with three areas of philosophical enquiry: truth, beauty, and goodness. These came to be instituted as logic, aesthetics, and ethics respectively. Logic tries to answer the question: How do you know that a statement is true? This assumes that every statement is capable of being categorized as true or false. But you cannot look at a great painting or listen to a great piece of music and ask whether it is true or not: the appropriate question is whether it is beautiful or not. How do you judge a piece of beauty? That is what aesthetics tries to do. Last, ethics address goodness: How do you know whether what you are doing is right (not legal, but right, in an ethical sense)? Is this judgement entirely personal, or is it relative to the group or society in which you live and work, or is it a product of some universal rules? These are the issues dealt with in the field of ethics.

Why does society have moral standards at all? First, they are (at least thought to be) of material consequence to society's well-being. It lays down a set of rules (or norms) of behaviour that are more than the *laws* that govern behaviour. Second, moral standards have a certain degree of permanence, immutability, or at least greater longevity than laws that are enacted by a group of persons at a point of time. Moral standards are not established by any legislative bodies, and often they are not codified; they evolve through a process of consensus in society. Third, moral standards provide a defence against the blatant exercise of self-interest. Thus if a person has a moral obligation to do something, he has to do it even though it may not be in his (at least immediate) self-interest. In extreme situations, taking a moral position may even invite death; yet the person takes it because he feels obliged to do so.

These considerations are, in the long run, expected to lead to a better society. In the case of business, better ethics may even mean better business, as I discuss later in this chapter.

ETHICAL JUDGEMENTS ARE NECESSARILY NORMATIVE

Ethics necessarily leads to normative judgements and is also dependant on the values of the persons making them. When you say that 'X is a cheat: he regularly fudges his travel bills to the company', you make an evaluative judgement because you feel such fudging is wrong. You pass such a judgement not necessarily because it is greatly harmful to the company (it may not be so; indeed it may be small amounts that really do not matter), but you form a value judgement that it is *wrong* to do this, even though its consequences may be insignificant. If you follow up with another sentence, 'Hence X should be sacked', you are clearly making a normative statement and you express your conviction that such behaviour *ought to* be punished.

All normative statements are not ethical. If you say, 'X should work harder', it involves no ethical overtones. If X decides not to work harder and is willing to accept the consequences, there is nothing more to be said, at least at an ethical level.

BUSINESS ETHICS

Business ethics is merely ethics applied in a business context. Ethics is ultimately personal, inasmuch as it is individuals who take decisions, and they are guided in these decisions based on their value systems. But they are applied in a business context. Business ethics as a field of study concerns itself about how moral standards apply to the conduct of organizations and individuals involved in these organizations. Business ethics is thus applied ethics, ethics applied to business.

Study of business ethics involves analysis of moral principles and norms, and how they are applied to specific situations by the people in companies. The prime reason why business ethics has come into such prominence lately is that all too often, businesses are seen to act in their self-interest, overriding accepted and acceptable moral standards. In the process, they bring about serious consequences to a large number of people in no way involved in their decisions. Recent corporate scandals have led to the realization that mere regulation, though essential, is not enough; corporate executives need to act morally and ethically, on their own, and willingly.

I do not argue that business ethics is separate from personal ethics. Indeed, organizations do not take decisions; only individuals do. They, however, take these decisions in a certain context, and this needs application of the principles in a different way, the main difference being that while in personal decisions, the decision maker alone (or at the most, his family) bears the consequences, in a business or organizational context, many others do.

CAN BUSINESS BE RUN ETHICALLY AT ALL?

No one, of course, says openly that he runs a business unethically. But statements such as 'Business is, after all business', and 'You can't be squeaky clean while running a business' reflect a mindset that shows that, to put it mildly, ethical considerations take a backseat in relation to business. In a hyper-competitive world, it may be argued, while others are not acting ethically, how can you do so? For example, a businessman may say, 'If my competitors are not using anti-pollution measures and are discharging their effluents into rivers, though I know this is unethical, I have to follow suit; if I install anti-pollution measures, it may push my costs up and I shall no longer be competitive.' It is the same when talking about tax evasion.

It must be noted that such considerations apply even in personal life, and you have to take a call on what you should do. For example, in a competitive MBA programme, if others are getting better grades through unfair means (such as copying from the internet and passing it off as their own), should you also do so, or stick to your own values and risk getting lower grades and, probably, a less glamorous job? I argue that though there may not be a universally applicable 'correct' answer, you need to develop your own moral compass and be guided by it. Developing a moral compass and a set of values is ultimately a question of development of character. The character of a person is how ultimately others see the person, and it affects the relationships others have with him.

The same applies to corporations as well. Each corporation develops a distinct identity or 'character' over a period of time. Some are 'good' and 'trustworthy' companies; others are not. These perceptions are shaped by the company's actions in the past, from the responses it has made at its defining moments. A well-regarded corporation has a different set of relationships with its stakeholders compared to one that has a poor reputation. The foremost among these is the development of trust, which is a valuable business asset.

CAN BUSINESS BE BETTER OFF BEING ETHICAL?

Is being ethical good for business? Can a business actually be *better off* being ethical? Can it do well by being good?

Even from a purely 'business' point of view, it may be a good policy to be ethical. Consider the following:

(i) Being ethical increases credibility.

Like trust, credibility is an essential ingredient of leadership. A leader needs to convince his followers about the need for believing in his pronouncements. The leader lifts the followers to a different level of energy. This cannot be done if the followers do not believe in what the leader says. The same applies to the organization's dealings with its customers, suppliers, and other stakeholders. A clever manager may be able to pick holes in a contract and even win cases in the courts, but these victories do not replace the loss of credibility the organization suffers. Credibility also enhances the trust investors have in the firm and enables them to place greater faith in the firm's pronouncements.

(ii)   Being ethical generates trust.

Trust acts as an invisible cost reducer. It reduces what are called transaction costs. A simple example of a transaction cost is the need to draw up elaborate contracts involving large costs by way of fees to lawyers and the time of management. Much of the terms of these contracts refer to what to do in situations when one of the parties does not act the way it is expected to. Then there are costs of enforcement in courts of law. A relationship based on trust, on the other hand, does not need such elaborate contracts. If the parties abide by the terms of contract, the trust is justified and the next round is still easier.

Business alliances, for example, need trust more than rigid contracts for their success. Research shows the crucial role trust plays in the success of alliances. Trust implies an understanding of the spirit of the agreement rather than the letter. Imagine a joint venture that starts with distrust of the real intentions of each party by the other party. Clearly, each party will take protective action 'just in case', and the joint venture will never achieve its potential. On the other hand, a company such as Infosys, reputed for its ethics, can negotiate better terms from its potentiality.

Consider the importance of trust in a consulting firm. Much confidential information is invariably given by a client to a consultant, and the client depends on the ability of the consultant to keep this data confidential. Similarly, the recommendations of a consultant need to be professional and not merely reflecting what the top management wishes the consultant to say, just as is the case with doctors and lawyers.

Trust applies within the organization as well. Indeed, trust is an essential part of leadership (Manikutty and Singh, 2009). To be a true leader, the followers need to have trust in their leader, and this alone can generate commitment. An unethical leader is viewed with suspicion, and the employees discount his words accordingly. Indeed, the top management is generally *not* trusted by the organization, distrust being the default state. Trust is a fragile emotion to be built up, and a single unethical act of the leader serves as a permanent seed of distrust. Commitment is broken, and the top management responds with increased controls and monitoring, setting in motion a costly and vicious cycle.

Trust and credibility are, of course, closely related, but not the same. A person's words and actions are credible if people think the words and actions match his thoughts; he means what he says. On the other hand, trust is bestowed on a person completely: 'He is trustworthy.' People stop being just logical with him and asking him why he is doing what he is doing; they assume that as their leader, he will do what is right and needed in a situation on their behalf. They feel they will not be cheated at some date. Trust is a more encompassing form of emotion than credibility.

BOX 1.1

The Case of the Angadias

The institution of angadias (local couriers) is an excellent example of trust-reducing transaction costs. These small-time couriers, especially in Gujarat and Mumbai, carry large amounts of cash, jewellery, and precious metals in person for delivery, with no documents other than scribbled notes. The system is incredibly cheap and reliable, and works entirely on trust. There are established networks which do not readily admit outsiders. The notorious *hawala* transactions operate on the same principle.

> Usually, systems based on trust also provide for severe punishments when the trust is breached. An interesting aside: the criminal world seems to depend more on trust than the 'civil' world!

(iii)   Being ethical improves relationships with key stakeholders.

Increasingly, business as being merely an agency for shareholders is coming under criticism. It is being replaced by a 'stakeholders' model in which many other groups, including the community the company is located in and the broader society, are seen as affecting the way a business functions. One of the leading rayon companies of India was polluting a river heavily, making its water unusable. The company at first ignored the protests of the local community, but ultimately had to close down the plant. The notion that a company can function entirely independently of its neighbouring community is not valid. In a more famous case, Coca-Cola India encountered endless troubles with its plant at Plachimada, a village in Kerala, due to its alleged drawing out of excess groundwater (see Box 1.2).

BOX 1.2

The Global Village of Plachimada

Plachimada is a small village in Palakkad district, Kerala, very near the border with Tamil Nadu. It is right in the rain-shadow region and is generally short of water during most parts of the year. The Indian subsidiary of Coca-Cola set up a plant there to produce carbonated and non-carbonated soft drinks. The plant commenced operations in March 2000. Within a year, the company faced serious agitation from the villagers alleging overexploitation of groundwater by Coca-Cola. The plant had three production lines—a 600-bottles-per-minute (BPM) line for carbonated soft drinks (CSDs) filling in returnable glass bottles (RGBs); a 965-BPM line for CSDs filling in PET bottles; and a 160-BPM RGB line for a juice-based drink, Maaza. According to the NGOs which took up the agitation, Coca-Cola consumed 1.5 million litres of water per day, extracted from the underground sources through powerful pumps (the company claimed its requirements never exceeded 620,000 litres per day, but this is also large in a semi-arid region). This led, it was alleged, to water scarcity and depleting groundwater levels.

The cause was taken up actively by NGOs. The local panchayat cancelled the plant's operational licence. It also alleged the farmlands nearby were getting polluted with the sludge generated from the plant. The matter went to the Kerala High Court.

The fight of the local people against a mighty MNC like Coca-Cola attracted a lot of attention in the district and in the state of Kerala. Even when there was a drought in 2001 and 2002, the company was stated to have operated at full capacity. The sludge was given by Coca-Cola as a free-of-cost 'fertilizer' to the farmers, and an investigating BBC team found that the sludge, far from being a fertilizer, contained toxic chemicals. A study by the Kerala State Pollution Board confirmed the presence of harmful chemicals.

The stakes of Coca-Cola on this plant also were very high and it was not willing to give up the project quickly. It stayed on, employed PR agencies and organized seminars, but the general antipathy to the company remained.

The company was to pay only a small amount as registration fee for the borewells, and did not have to pay for the water as such. This added to the negative image of an MNC pumping out water at no cost, adding some ingredients, and selling it at a huge profit.

On March 8, 2004, the Kerala Government ordered the cessation of the plant's operations till June 15, 2004 (when the monsoon would arrive in Kerala). The case attracted a lot of global attention, and the cause was taken up by none other than Anita Roddick of The Body Shop fame. There was a devastating programme broadcast by BBC on the issue, and a number of newspapers such as *The Guardian*, *The Times*, and *The Financial Times* of the UK; *The New York Times* of the USA; *Le Monde* of France; and *Asahi Shimbun* of Japan joined the fray. The little village of Plachimada went global. On the whole, Coca-Cola seemed to come out in a poor light over the episode. Not only the Plachimada plant but the Coca-Cola company in India suffered a major hit. The Plachimada plant has not reopened till date.

Coca-Cola also encountered similar resistance and faced agitation in Kaladera, Rajasthan, in June 2004.

Source: Nantoo Banerjee, *The Real Thing: Coke's Bumpy Ride through India*, Kolkata: Frontpage Publications, 2009; http://www. goodnewsindia.com/index.php/Supplement/article/396/; http:// www.indiaresource.org/campaigns/coke/2004/heatison.html; Alexander Cockburn, 'How Coca Cola Gave Back to Plachimada', http://www.indiaresource.org/campaigns/coke/2004/heatison. html, all accessed on August 1, 2011. Some other related websites were also accessed.

Clearly, Coca-Cola, for whatever reason, did not think it important to open a meaningful dialogue with its community. It rather thought of what was within its legal rights and perhaps never thought that, with its battery of clever lawyers and its ability to influence the policymakers in Delhi, the poor and ill-informed villagers would really fight with it. It saw the courts as the solution to all its problems, and for the steps taken by the panchayats and the government its response was to fight the battle in the courts. In other words, its line of thinking was: What is the law? What are my rights? Is what I am doing legal? It seemed to care little for the community in which it operated and the problems it created for that community.

Irrespective of whether the actions of companies are just illegal or also unethical, the fact remains that they need the support of the community and, to counter political pressures, the support of the local governments as well. A company that is functioning with a hostile community around it is, at the end of the day, fighting a losing battle. Certainly the battle is hugely costly. Companies, at best, fight costly legal battles to survive and continue and, at worst, are forced to close down their operations at a considerable loss. If the companies pause to think not so much of the legality of their actions as their being 'right' or not, many of the problems may be avoided.

WHAT ROLE DOES THE TOP MANAGEMENT PLAY IN THE ETHICAL ORIENTATION OF AN ORGANIZATION?

Can the leader set standards of ethics in an organization? Or does the organization have a momentum of its own, which the leader can influence only to a limited extent?

This question is important because though it might seem that the leader has the power to set the ethical standards and to punish deviants, in reality this power may be much less than appears at first sight. In political leadership, we have recently witnessed leaders of impeccable personal integrity watching helplessly as the standards of morality and behaviour of those supposedly reporting to them descended to abysmally new lows. In organizations, too, there would be people of high personal integrity whose subordinates are blatantly unethical. How does the leader deal with them?

Jack Welch, CEO of GE for two decades, identified four types of managers (see Box 1.3). The hardest to deal are the Type-4 managers who are very smart and competent yet do not share the core values of the organization. In other words, they are the 'competent rogues'. It is easy to say that leaders must show the way by firing them, but in reality this may be difficult because these managers may be in crucial positions and may have with them many confidential pieces of information. But the leader comes across a defining moment sooner or later, and has to take a tough call.

BOX 1.3

Jack Welch's Four Types of Managers

Jack Welch identified four types of managers along two dimensions: competence and their values. Dealing with Type-1 managers may be easy: Show them the door.

Type-3 managers are also easy to deal with: Hold fast to them—they are the gems. Type-2 managers have the right values but lack competencies. They can be trained and some positions can be found where they can have a better fit, though in reality too many such persons cannot be retained in the organization. Type-4 managers are the hardest to deal with—and the most difficult to identify. They may appear to be dedicated, honest, and sincere but may be resorting to shortcuts and compromises to achieve their objectives. In such cases, leaders need to question when

---

someone is producing a *particularly good* result consistently because they may be resorting to shortcuts and unethical practices. If Type-4 managers are identified, probably they need to be told about it, and most likely they will not improve, but merely make their operations more difficult to detect. They need to be marked and shown the door at an appropriate time. They are like cancer cells that quickly infect other members of the organization.

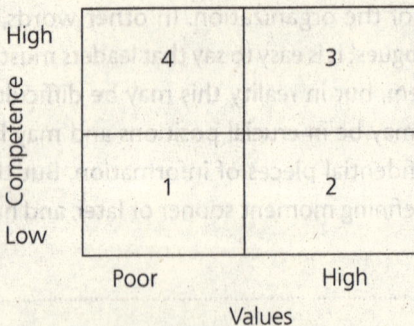

Source: 'GE's Two-Decade Transformation: Jack Welch's Leadership', Harvard Business School Case #9-399-150, Boston, MA: Harvard Business School, Harvard University.

Matters get complicated when the members of the top management, including members of the board of directors have their own compensation packages tied up to the results of the company, and they become interested only in earning profits and not in how these profits are made. This is what happened with Barings Bank in the early 1990s, when a rogue trader, Nick Leeson, managed to produce unbelievable (fictitious) profits day after day, and the board never seriously questioned how he was doing it. The company results and their own bonuses, tied to these results, were becoming good as well, and no one had the motivation to check whether there was anything amiss. Leeson was exposing the bank to high risks until one day the well-regarded bank collapsed. It went bankrupt and was sold for £1 in 1995.

It is certainly true that leaders must set standards and show themselves as exemplars. After all, the saying goes, '*Yatha Raja, thatha praja*,' that is, 'As is the King, so are the subjects'. But that may not be enough. The leader also needs to set up such systems and control so that at different levels of the organization, violations are detected and curbed. In parallel, the leader needs to set up a culture of honesty, where members of the organization willingly subscribe to a code of conduct, not because of control and compulsion, but because they feel committed towards it. Each member becomes a leader, a custodian of the organizational values and defends them against onslaughts, even if they arise from the leader himself.

PERSONAL ETHICS VERSUS ORGANIZATIONAL ETHICS

What is the link between personal ethics (especially those of the leaders and the top management) and the business ethics of the organization? What role does the development of character play in the preparation for leadership positions?

Ultimately, ethics start at an individual level. It will be one of the themes in this book that, ultimately, you have to develop your own codes of ethics, find your own moral compass. Ken Blanchard and Spencer Johnson in their famous book *One Minute Manager* (1983) simplified the problem by prescribing the 'mirror test'. They ask the following questions: Can you look at yourself in the mirror and feel reassured that there is nothing you have done that you need to be ashamed of? Can you bear to look at your own face?

This test, however, is highly oversimplified. People continue to do many things and rationalize their actions in some way or other: 'Everyone does it', 'It has to be done in this business', and so on. They develop psychological defence mechanisms to convince themselves that they are right, or quote scriptures to prove that even the divinities did it.

The challenge is to develop your own moral compass and decide what you should do, and be clear as to why you are doing it that way. It is a mix of reasoning and an intuitive understanding of the right thing to do, what may be called using your 'moral sense'. This book will take you through the process of developing this reasoning and moral sense, but it must be emphasized that such issues can never be analysed fully. You need to develop an ability to understand what the true problem is and arrive at a holistic solution.

There are really no 'solutions' to these problems; there can be only *your own* solutions. Hopefully such a study will provide a framework not for getting the answers, but for developing the right questions to ask.

CONCLUSION

In this chapter, I have discussed the basic concept of ethics, and how business ethics add more dimensions to personal ethics. Corporations are here to stay and will be more and more accountable. They are being scrutinized increasingly based also on the ethical dimensions, not merely on the profits they make.

I discussed the nature of ethics and what ethics is all about, and raised the question of whether business can be better off (in a business sense) being ethical. I argued that managers, and especially the top management, play a key role not only in behaving ethically themselves, but in creating an ethical climate in the organization. Finally, I briefly looked at different dimensions of corporate ethics.

I argued that to arrive at the answer to the question, 'Is what I am doing right/moral?' there is a need for a logical reasoning process as a component. To enable such reasoning, it is necessary to understand the rudiments of what we call 'theories' of ethics. I look at some of the important theories in the next chapter.

KEY TAKEAWAYS

(1) Ethics is the study of understanding whether what we do is good and right.

(2) Business ethics is a subset of ethics in general.

(3) Even though it is individuals who take decisions, they do so under a framework laid down by corporations, and hence business or corporate ethics becomes a separate field of study.

(4) It is assumed that business *can* and *should be* run ethically, and I plan to present you with the issues involved, and develop a framework on how to do it on your own.

(5) Running a business ethically may be better in the long run for the business because:

    a. it enhances the credibility of the management;

    b. it enhances the trust reposed in the management; and

    c. it can reduce costs, especially the transaction costs involved in drawing up elaborate contracts and fighting expensive court battles.

(6) The top management plays a role in creating an ethical climate in the organization and sending the right signals.

REFERENCES

Banerjee, N. 2009. *The Real Thing: Coke's Bumpy Ride through India*. Kolkata: Frontpage Publications.

Blanchard, K. and S. Johnson. 1983. *The One Minute Manager*. London: Willow Books.

Cockburn, A. 2004, 'How Coca Cola Gave Back to Plachimada'. http://www.indiaresource.org/campaigns/coke/2004/heatison.html, accessed on August 1, 2011.

Das, G. 2010. *The Difficulty of Being Good: On the Subtle Art of Dharma*. New Delhi: Allen Lane/Penguin Books.

'GE's Two-decade Transformation: Jack Welch's Leadership'. 1999. Harvard Business School Case #9-399-150. Boston, MA: Harvard Business School, Harvard University.

Friedman, M. 1970. 'The Social Responsibility of Business is to Increase its Profits'. *The New York Times Magazine*. September 13.

Manikutty, S. and S.P. Singh. 2009. *The Essentials of Leadership*. New Delhi: Macmillan.

'The Plachimada Promise', news item, June 19, 2005, taken from http://www.goodnewsindia.com/index.php/Supplement/article/396/ accessed on August 1, 2011.

Surendranath, C. 2004. 'Coke vs. People: Heat is on Plachimada'. http://www.indiaresource.org/campaigns/coke/2004/heatison.html, accessed on August 1, 2011.

reasoned conclusion.

2

Can We Analyse Ethical Issues?

'He who loves practice without theory is like the sailor who boards
a ship without a rudder and compass and never knows where he
may cast.'

—Leonardo da Vinci

From Chapter 1, it should be obvious to the reader that ethical
questions are complex. All too often ethical issues are dealt with
summarily, almost like saying, 'Because I say so'. Can you analyse
an ethical issue in a way that you arrive at some kind of *reasoned*
conclusion, a conclusion that you can justify to others? The
objective of this chapter is to point to some ways of doing
this, with the caveat that this is not like solving a mathematical
problem with a single solution. In fact, there could be multiple
'right' answers.

In order to adopt such a reasoning, you should be familiar with
what may be called 'theories' of ethics. These, in reality, are the
outcomes of the thinking of different philosophers who tried to
grapple with the basic question, 'How do you know that what you
are doing is right?' I shall briefly review these different theories
and present you with a set of questions you can ask while trying
to answer an ethical problem. These questions can highlight the
different dimensions of an ethical problem, and though you may

not reach a deterministic conclusion, you can at least reach a reasoned conclusion.

Consider the following example in Box 2.1 which shows how reasoning can be applied to such a problem, and how adopting different approaches can lead to different processes of reasoning and to different solutions.

BOX 2.1

The Case of Dying Fish

Zuari Agrochemicals was a Birla group company that set up a fertilizer plant in the ecologically sensitive coast of Goa in the early 1970s. At that time, India was grappling with the problem of acute shortage of fertilizers, affecting food production. Import was also difficult due to shortage of foreign exchange. Hence the fertilizer plant set up served a vital national need.

The plant went into production in June 1973. Its effluents were discharged into the sea at a distance from the coast. In September 1973, it was reported that the incidence of dead fish from the sea in the vicinity of the discharge from the plant was higher than usual. The company claimed that its effluents were within the norms for pollution set by the government and that it had obtained collaboration for the design and construction of the plant from a reputed Japanese firm. Increase in the incidence of dead fish could have been due to many reasons, including natural oceanic phenomena. Different committees set up by the government to go into the problem posed by Zuari came up with different results.

Soon after the dead fish problem, the company faced a problem on another front. Its ammonia effluents were discharged into a reservoir and, in December 1974, the villages around the

---

reservoir and surrounding the factory alleged that there was seepage from these tanks resulting in damage to the soil, to the crops, and to their drinking water sources. The company again denied that it had anything to do with the problem, but it offered to assist the villagers with drinking water. However, the protests by the villagers continued, alleging withering of crops due to ammonia contamination. They wanted nothing short of the closure of the plant.

There were better ways to control pollution more effectively, but these involved the installation of additional equipment that was quite expensive. The cost of the fertilizers produced would increase, imposing a general cost on the economy.

Source: 'The Case of the Dying Fish', Case #BP 143, Indian Institute of Management, Ahmedabad, Gujarat.

What should the company have done? In such a situation, one manager might reason as follows:

If we install the best pollution control devices available, the damage to the fish and the seepage problems could probably be contained. But then it may not, because the death of the fish could be due to various oceanic phenomena (as was suggested in one report) and if it is indeed so, then the additional measures would be for nothing. The farmers could be agitating simply to get some compensation from the company. We could negotiate with the farmers and fishermen and could compensate them for damages but then the demands would simply escalate. One sure outcome of these measures, however, would be an increase in the costs of the fertilizers to be produced. Responding to the call for closure would aggravate the fertilizer shortage in the country, with consequences for food production, and would affect a large number of people.

Hence I would go by the principle of 'the greatest good for the greatest number'. This clearly is *not* served by closing the plant, and hence I would not close the plant under any circumstances. I would not like to add to the cost by installing additional pollution control equipment, affecting the numerous farmers in the country who would have to pay more for the fertilizers. For all I know, even if I install additional equipment, the farmers and fishermen may still continue the protests in the hope of extracting some more compensation. Hence I shall ignore the call of the villagers and fishermen, and urge the government to put down the protests. After all, the damages, if any, to a few farmers and fishermen would be more than compensated by the increase in benefits to the consumers of fertilizers and food. If any real damage is proved by the farmers or the fishermen, I would compensate them for that.

A second manager might reason thus:

Serving the stockholders is my primary duty. I might also look at my duties towards others—my employees, my customers, and the community. I shall also look at these different stakeholders and balance my duties.

If I install the pollution control devices, surely my shareholders would be affected. If I close down the plant, the shareholders, the employers (many of whom were also villagers from the same villages), and the farmers in the country who need fertilizers will be affected. If I do nothing, the community will be affected.

Though I have duties to all the above, my *primary* duty is to shareholders, then to my employees, and then to my consumers. Hence my decision is to do nothing, since that would be the best for the shareholders.

Note that though the conclusions of the two managers may be the same, the processes of arriving at them are quite different. In the first formulation, there is no concept of duty (which has a moral connotation in itself), but only of utility, more specifically, economic utility. In the second formulation, the dominant criterion for the decision is based on the concept of a duty, an obligation, which goes beyond pure economic considerations.

A third manager may adopt an entirely different approach and arrive at a different conclusion:

As the manager of this plant, it is not enough for me to confront the economic consequences or the consequences of applying what, in essence, is a narrow concept of duty. I have certain moral obligations that are absolute. Depriving any group of people of their livelihood is wrong, especially when I can clearly identify these people and the consequences they suffer as a result of my actions. On the other hand, the people who may benefit are uncertain; after all, the government or the company itself could set up another fertilizer plant somewhere else.

If I pose this as an abstract problem to anyone, without reference to the specifics of the company or the situation, virtually everyone would answer that it is unethical to deprive a group of people of their livelihood, even though many others might benefit.

Hence, I shall do whatever is needed to eliminate the damages caused to the environment, even though it may lead to increase in costs. I do not presume that the farmers and fishermen are unreasonable and would continue to agitate, because they also have a sense of moral values. I would take such steps as to make sure that the factory has, at the very least, an impact that is neutral, that is, no one is worse off as a result of this plant.

Here the reasoning is completely different. It focuses on certain universal principles (do not deprive *any section of* people of their livelihood) that cannot be compromised. In effect, a group of persons who, at present, are not getting any benefits, but will benefit due to an action, is not the same as depriving someone else who is already getting the benefits. There are some core principles that define the basics of what it means to be human and are considered inviolable.

Each of the above three processes of reasoning introduces us to three different types of ethical reasoning: (i) consequentialism, which focuses on consequences; (ii) in terms of duties and obligations and their prioritization; and (iii) a set of categorical imperatives. I will briefly look at these theories (for a more detailed discussion of these approaches, see Thomas Donaldson and Patricia H. Werhane, 1983).

CONSEQUENTIALISM OR UTILITARIANISM

This approach evaluates the ethics of an action based purely on the consequences, or the increase/decrease in utility to all who reap the consequences of the action. Hence this approach is also considered teleological (derived from the Greek word *telos*, meaning 'end' or 'purpose'). In one version of this approach, it looks at what is the best for *me*, that is, for the doer, and hence is called ethical egoism. It may be what is best for a corporation as well (the so-called maximization-of-profits approach). Such a comparison of alternatives needs a common currency, and the easiest one to adopt is cash, or economic value.

This approach has its problems, since a sum of, say, Rs 1000, for a poor person may not be of the same value to a very rich person. Hence economists replaced the purely monetary value with an abstract concept called utility. This is, however, difficult to measure. In its pure form, this approach is largely abandoned now, since it seeks to maximize the satisfaction derived from achieving your ends, however ignoble they may be. It is also called the utilitarian approach and its best known proponents were the economists Jeremy Bentham and John Stuart Mill. This version looks at the maximization of overall good, defined in terms of whoever is affected. Stated in a simple way, the theory aims for the greatest good for the largest number. You put a value for the utility for each person who is affected and then add it up (this is called the utility function), then this is sought to be maximized.

The main problem with this approach is that it completely neglects the aspect of justice. Any degree of injustice to a minority is acceptable if it improves the welfare of the majority. This underlies the discussions on dams and certain industrial and mining projects that involve displacement of people. The problems Sterlite encountered in Niyamgiri, Tata Motors encountered in

Singur, and other companies encountered in SEZs (Special Economic Zones), thermal power plants, etc. have this kind of issue at the core: Can major consequences to the lives of some people be accepted, even for the welfare of a much larger number? To understand the limitations of such an approach, consider the following interesting situation I have posed to the students in many of my classes:

> ## BOX 2.2
>
> ### Can You Solve this One? Dilemma #1
>
> Imagine a casualty ward in a hospital. Three emergency victims are brought in. They will surely die unless some organs are quickly transplanted. One needs a liver transplant; the second, a kidney transplant (both kidneys); and the third, a heart transplant. These organs are not available readily, but immediate surgery is essential for all three if they are to survive.
>
> There is a patient waiting for consultation in the outpatient ward for common cold. A nurse has a bright idea. Why not kill this person, take out his organs and transplant them to the three patients? After all, only one man dies; but three lives are saved.
>
> *Source:* Adapted from Marc Hauser (2006), *The Moral Minds*, New York: HarperCollins, p. 32.

To every class that I have posed this problem, the vast majority do not support what they see as the bizarre reasoning of the nurse (what I find remarkable is that there *are* invariably some, a few, who actually support such an action as well). Yet in purely consequentialist terms, her reasoning is justified. Saving three lives at the expense of one is justified, *generally*. Yet few would actually accept the nurse's idea and kill the outpatient. It will not be considered ethical.

But consider the problem outlined in Box 2.3.

Again, just as in the case of the accident victims and the nurse, few, but invariably more than in the first example, would vote for switching the points to the main line, even though such a switching would involve saving the lives of three people, while sacrificing only one. Interestingly, if it were forty people in the loop line rather than three, many more would approve of the switching, even though no one would be able to say when his decision would change, and why. Would they change at five? Ten? Twenty, maybe? Why this number?

The majority, however, would not feel that it is ethical to save the lives of three and sacrifice that of one in this case. Strangely, most would not find it easy to articulate *why* they feel that it is wrong to do so. (What is your own decision as regards these two cases? What is your reasoning behind this decision?) But after some introspection, they would reach the conclusion that, in both examples, they have employed a reasoning based not on utility, but justice at its core. You feel that it is *unjust* to kill the unsuspecting person waiting in the outpatient ward or the person who is walking on the main line because he has reason to believe that he is safe doing so (trains do not generally come on this line). But consider the following example:

BOX 2.4

Can You Solve this One? Dilemma #3

There is a boat which is crossing a turbulent river in the monsoon season. It is carrying forty people instead of its capacity of thirty. Suddenly, midstream, the boat develops a leak. But it can be saved if ten people are pushed into the river. They will be chosen at random and, once pushed, death is certain. If this is not done, almost surely the boat will sink, and all forty lives would be lost. What should the captain of the boat do?

Here, though it again involves saving thirty lives and deliberately sacrificing only ten (the same ratio as in the nurse and the loop line examples), generally there is near unanimity: that in this situation, the pushing of ten people is justified, *so long as they are chosen at random.* If they are not, as happens in the famous scene in the film *The Titanic*, you feel a sense of outrage. (In this scene, the ship will sink soon, and the number of lifeboats available on board is not enough. So the deck class passengers are locked up and left to drown to save the lives of higher class passengers).

Consider, yet again, the dilemma in Box 2.5.

BOX 2.5

Can You Solve this One? Dilemma #4

Suppose that in the example given in Box 2.4 before, the boat is not leaking and there is no danger to the boat, but five more people, swept in the river, grab the boat and implore to be taken into it. Not taking them would be sure death for all five, but taking them would put the entire forty, as well as the new five, at a high risk, indeed a near certainty of drowning.

In this situation, initially few would approve of taking the additional five.

Thus consequentialism and utilitarianism clearly operate in a context. What are superficially two similar situations in fact turn out to be different. But if you ask the question what *is* different in the situation, the respondents are confused and cannot put their finger on the difference.

BOX 2.6

How did you respond to each of the dilemmas? What is the difference in the situations posed by the dilemmas?

I shall return to this question a little later.

CONSEQUENTIALISM: THE CHECKLIST OF QUESTIONS

To arrive at a reasoned answer through the consequentialist or utilitarian approach, you can proceed on the lines of reasoning below:

1. What are the options open to me?

2. In each option, who is affected? Positively? Negatively? By how much?

3. If I add up the net consequences under each option, which option gives the best overall outcome?

4. Select that option.

THE DUTY, RIGHTS, AND JUSTICE PERSPECTIVE AND HUMANISM

In this perspective, every human being in society has some rights and some duties. There may be multiple duties towards multiple groups of persons as, for example, towards your family, employees, customers, community, and so on. You as the decision maker must order these duties in a hierarchical fashion, starting from the most important. This is to be done without having any specific situation in mind, or 'under a veil of ignorance'. Depending on how you arrange these duties in your order of priority, the 'right thing to do' can be found: that action is right which discharges your duties towards the most important stakeholder(s). This ordering guides one as to what to do in a given situation.

Laws are passed employing this principle. They are first passed to be applied generally, without having any specific person or group of persons in mind, and are applied in specific situations to judge whether any person is guilty and what punishment would be appropriate.

It is generally agreed that parents must act in the best interests of their children. But suppose an accused is brought before a judge for a heinous murder, and it turns out that it is his son. If the judge discharges his son simply for his being his son, most of us would not agree that the judge has acted ethically. His duty as a judge must precede that of a parent. He failed in getting his priorities right.

What appears to be a rather straightforward case as related above, when applied to a business context becomes more difficult. The agency theory in corporate governance views managers as agents of shareholders, and argues that their *sole* duty is towards the shareholders. This is the essence of Milton Friedman's argument referred to in Chapter 1. The proponents of this view argue that managers basically use the funds given to them by shareholders, and are hence expected to use them in such a way that the shareholders get the maximum benefit. Not doing so is unethical and a betrayal of trust. In other words, the first priority of the manager is the shareholder group.

This view leaves each decision maker to decide what his priorities are. There are no guidelines for this. Take, for example, the principle that in the military or paramilitary forces, one should carry out the orders of the superiors. Doing so will enable better defence of the country, and hence is good for the country. Blind application of this principle, however, can lead to horrific consequences as, for example, in the case of Nazi concentration camps where each followed orders from his superior to do things which would presumably benefit the fatherland in the long run. The principle of obedience to orders from someone higher in hierarchy was applied mindlessly, as an absolute principle (see also Box 10.1 in Chapter 10). In the same manner, a manager may fire a subordinate on 'orders from above' even though he knows that this is an unfair and unjust act, in the interests of 'organization discipline'. People are reduced to machines obeying orders, not exercising any judgement.

To deal with this dilemma, the concept of duty is replaced by justice, fairness, and a sense of humanism. *Any* priorities will not do; they must have the sanction of society and must conform to certain other norms such as fairness and justice.

THE DUTIES, RIGHTS, AND JUSTICE APPROACH: THE CHECKLIST OF QUESTIONS

To arrive at a reasoned answer through the approach outlined above, you can proceed on the lines of reasoning given below:

1. Who is affected by my action?
2. What is my duty towards each person? What are my priorities?
3. If I apply these priorities, does this lead to any injustice or unfairness?
4. Act as per the duties set out in item (2) above, unless the answer to item (3) is yes. In that case, modify to eliminate unfairness.

THEORY OF MORAL INSTINCTS

This approach, largely attributed to the philosopher John Rawls, essentially argues that all human beings are born with a moral sense, a moral instinct. In a series of remarkable experiments, even babies as young as one-and-a-half years were seen to have developed a sense of right and wrong, fair and unfair actions. They are not completely self-centred, as was earlier believed by some psychologists. In his remarkable book *Moral Minds: How Nature Designed Our Universal Sense of Right and Wrong* (2006), Marc Hauser gives numerous examples of how people develop their moral instincts from the time they were babies. In short, he concludes that people can *intuitively* sense what is right and what is wrong and the reasoning and emotions follow. The moral judgements are arrived at through 'unconscious and inaccessible principles'.

This is a persuasive argument, but leads to the conclusion that by no training programmes or by reading any books (including this one), can you hope to achieve a better ethical capability. But it could be developed by consciously rewiring your brain through active reflection. In other words, it is all up to you.

Evidently, this formulation has its own problems. There may be persons who are psychopaths or are somewhat abnormal, and they may make horrific decisions based on their wrong moral instincts. These people may *appear* normal but in fact might have serious mental problems, including a total lack of conscience. Unfortunately, they may occupy managerial positions, including senior ones, and may make terrible decisions affecting many seriously.

THE MORAL–INSTINCTS APPROACH: THE CHECKLIST OF QUESTIONS

To arrive at a reasoned answer through the moral–instincts approach, you can proceed on the lines of reasoning given below:

1. Let me look at the different courses of action open to me holistically. Which ones sound right to me? Which ones sound wrong to me?

2. *Having identified which ones I find right or wrong,* I analyse why.

3. I choose the one which appears to be right to me intuitively, and among the right courses, the one with the best outcome.

THE MORAL DILEMMAS REVISITED

Let us now revisit the accident victims, the outpatient and the nurse. Even though it may appear to be 'economically' justified to kill one person and save three, why do most people feel it is wrong to kill the outpatient? Note that despite the reasoning that they may offer later, people make their first judgement *instinctively*, rather than logically. On reflection, many respondents may answer that such killing of one person is not acceptable because the victim is not given a *choice* in this matter. The victim is in no way responsible for the accident or its consequences. If he *volunteers* to be killed and donate the organs, there is much less of an ethical dilemma. But if he is killed unsuspectingly, his right as a human being is violated, while the other three have no such *right in this situation*, since they have, however it may be, got involved in the accident. But in the case of the boat, the ten persons selected at random are *informed* of the situation, and all are given an equal chance to survive. The survivors are not violating the right to life of the others (chosen to die) in any way. If five of them volunteer to jump off the boat, they forsake the rights, and there is no dilemma at all. It is the same with regard to the five caught up in the stream and requesting to enter the boat. While it would be nice to let them in, they have no *right* to be let in, while those in the boat have a right to be carried safely. Thus the letting in of the five violates the rights of those in the boat.

In all the examples above, I am not going by what maximizes utility, but by what is *just*. The fact that there is a near unanimity in the verdicts of what is to be done in each case shows that despite not having any exposure to any theories of ethics, people do have a moral instinct. While the application in specific situations may lead to perverse decisions, at least this approach has an advantage of consistency.

Ethics and justice cannot be separated. Blind justice may be cruel and if the laws under which the justice is dispensed are themselves oppressive, unjust, and unethical, there is not much to be said for that justice. But ethics without justice has serious problems as a concept.

THE DOCTRINE OF CATEGORICAL IMPERATIVE

This is the perspective most religions take: Certain things are wrong in whatever circumstances. There are the ten commandments in the Bible (see Box 2.7).

> **BOX 2.7**
>
> The Ten Commandments
>
> The Ten Commandments are found in the Bible's Old Testament in *Exodus*, Chapter 20. According to the Bible, they were given directly by God to the people of Israel at Mount Sinai after He had delivered them from slavery in Egypt. They go as follows:

> *And God spoke all these words, saying: 'I am the LORD your God...*
>
> ONE: *You shall have no other gods before Me.*
>
> TWO: *You shall not make for yourself a carved image—any likeness of anything that is in heaven above, or that is in the earth beneath, or that is in the water under the earth.*
>
> THREE: *You shall not take the name of the LORD your God in vain.*
>
> FOUR: *Remember the Sabbath day, to keep it holy.*
>
> FIVE: *Honour your father and your mother.*
>
> SIX: *You shall not murder.*
>
> SEVEN: *You shall not commit adultery.*
>
> EIGHT: *You shall not steal.*
>
> NINE: *You shall not bear false witness against your neighbour.*
>
> TEN: *You shall not covet your neighbour's house; you shall not covet your neighbour's wife nor his male servant, nor his female servant, nor his ox, nor his donkey, nor anything that is your neighbour's.'*

Viewed by themselves, they seem to be perfectly valid and seem to offer guidelines for ethical conduct. You can view your actions against these universal edicts. After all, who can argue in favour of killing or stealing?

The famous German philosopher Immanuel Kant pursued this line with his doctrine of the 'categorical imperative'. There are certain principles which are in the nature of absolute dictates that you must follow. They are what he calls 'universal laws of action' which, if everyone observes them, will eventually lead to a better society. These laws can be discovered by each individual through a process of reasoning. For example, a world in which everyone steals from one another is clearly not a desirable world to live in. Hence 'not stealing' is a categorical imperative.

But universal application of this principle to all situations, like many of the principles of the Ten Commandments, leads to serious difficulties. Supposing on a road, you find a robber about to kill an innocent person, with a motive to rob him. You have a gun yourself. Are you justified in killing the robber? (Note that I am not talking of legal culpability, but the ethics of the action). You can prevent the death of an innocent person and will kill only a murderer.

Even if there are some divided opinions on this, supposing you substitute the innocent stranger with your wife or brother. Suddenly there is near unanimity on what should be done. Clearly, the context affects the rules of the game; categorical imperatives are not that categorical after all.

Generally, there would be unanimous agreement that bribing is not a good practice. But sometimes it becomes hard to pronounce a clear judgement. Take the case of the Lockheed scandal (see Box 2.8). The German industrialist Oskar Schindler saved the lives of many Jews by bribing Gestapo men and prison guards during the Nazi era. Would you approve of this bribery?

BOX 2.8

The Lockheed Scandal

In 1972, the executives of the aircraft manufacturing firm Lockheed Corporation, USA, badly needed orders since the company was in dire straits. There was a prospective order from a Japanese airline for six wide-bodied tri-star jets and the order was hotly contested by all leading airplane manufacturers. The trouble was that it was conveyed to the Lockheed manager, Carl

---

Kotchian, who, in his discussion on the deal, had agreed that a substantial bribe needed to be paid to get the order. Other airlines were willing to do it. If the order was not secured, there was a strong possibility of Lockheed Corporation going bankrupt, affecting its shareholders and throwing a large number of employees out of work.

What should Kotchian do?

Source: Adapted from 'Case Study: Lockheed Aircraft Corporation', in T. Donaldson and P.H. Werhane (eds), *Ethical Issues in Business: A Philosophical Approach*, Englewoods Cliffs, NJ: Prentice Hall, 1983.

This difficult situation was indeed faced, and apart from the ethical aspects, it was also *illegal* to participate in such bribing, as per US law. But if Kotchian refused to bribe, would he be shirking his duty towards the organization, to its shareholders and employees? Would he be responsible for the resultant loss of jobs, and possibly for some of the shareholders losing their savings?

This illustration also brings up another issue: Are the standards of ethics the same in all societies? What if, in Japan, such bribing was the *usual* accepted way of doing business? This brings me to a modified approach of the categorical imperative called ethical relativism.

ETHICAL RELATIVISM

From this perspective, all ethical standards are relative, that is, they are products of the culture of the region or country. What is ethical in one country or one society may be considered unethical in another country or society. Ultimately, ethical judgements are all value judgements, and values are relative and culture dependent.

For example, among Eskimos, when a person becomes very old and a burden on others, when he can no longer hunt, cook, or do anything productive, it is considered perfectly ethical to send him away to die. (Actually, the old person tells others that he is going 'hunting'. Everyone knows what that is, and no one objects or tries to dissuade him). In this society resources are very scarce, and there is not much scope for supporting redundant persons. Yet in India or China if anyone does the same thing, it would be considered despicable and inhuman. Indians and Chinese are expected to take care of their parents. It is considered unethical not to look after your parents in their old age and abandon them to their fate (though this attitude is, regrettably, changing fast).

It is the same with regard to bribery, gambling, cheating, or bluffing in some situations; for example, in some societies and countries, gambling and drinking are considered sinful (as, for example, in certain Muslim countries) whereas in others they may not. It is considered perfectly fine to bluff while playing poker or bridge; indeed, it is a part of the rules of the game. Negotiations involve some kind of bluffing as, for example, when one party says, 'This is the maximum I can offer' though in reality, he may be prepared to offer more. In some countries, copying by students may be considered cheating, while in others, it may be seen as helping out a weak student.

Though many actions and norms are indeed relative, there are some acts that are considered universally right or wrong. Not every act is relative. These may be called the categorical imperatives. For example, helping an accident victim or a person in distress is probably considered the right thing to do irrespective of the society you live in. Skinning newborn babies and eating them, or raping your mother would be considered disgusting and immoral in all societies. There *are* some universal rules, or at least some that command wide acceptance. These need to be discovered.

The bigger problem with this sort of relativism is that when the logic is pushed to its limits, the relativism stops only at an individual level. If ethical standards are relative, you cannot draw a line at, say, the level of state, district, or even village. Everyone can declare that this is *his* personal code of ethics. In such a society, everything is permitted; nothing is unethical. That is why Albert Einstein said, 'Relativity is for physics; it does not apply in ethics.'

Albert Camus's famous story *L'Etranger* (The Stranger, 1942) illustrates how society may view someone who sets his own moral standards.

BOX 2.9

L'Etranger (The Stranger)

Albert Camus's famous novel *L'Etranger* is about a person, Mauersault, who does not follow the accepted standards of society. He kills an Arab whom he knows, more in self-defence than with the actual intent to kill (the Arab flashed a knife at him), but having killed him with the first shot, follows it up with four more shots to the dead body. During the trial, the prosecutor relies more on the fact that when his mother died, Mauersault did not cry or exhibit any emotion, and indeed had some coffee beside her dead body. This, according to the prosecutor, shows that Mauersault is a 'soulless monster' and demands that a death sentence be pronounced. No one expects a death sentence, considering the circumstances the crime was committed in, but the jury finds him guilty and indeed a death sentence is passed

---

on him. Finally, Mauersault refuses the services of a chaplain saying that he does not believe in God, and has no remorse for anything he has done. Indeed, he has done nothing that requires him to feel remorse as such, but his odd standard of behaviour, especially his not having exhibited the emotions that were expected at his mother's funeral, leads the jury to pronounce him guilty and award him the death sentence.

THE DOCTRINE OF CATEGORICAL IMPERATIVE: THE CHECKLIST OF QUESTIONS

A person moving on the route of the categorical imperative may proceed on the lines of reasoning below:

1. With regard to the issue, what are the core values, the categorical imperatives that I must rely on? I arrive at them by universalizing the situation, and see whether, if all followed one alternative rather than the other, the world would be a better place to be in.

2. Can these imperatives be applied universally?

3. I accept the imperatives that, according to me, must ride supreme.

The best illustration of this approach is what Gandhi did after the Chauri Chaura incident, in which a mob burnt some policemen in a police station alive. The Civil Disobedience Movement was gaining momentum at this point. But to Gandhi, such violence was not acceptable as a means. Non-violence was a categorical imperative. Hence even though it would lead (and it did lead) to a setback to the movement, he was adamant about suspending the movement.

THE CONCEPT OF DHARMA

Before I conclude this chapter, I will look at how Indian philosophers viewed ethics. Unlike Western philosophers, Indian philosophers did not write down their thoughts in a comprehensive way, but many of the scriptures and puranas give a glimpse into their thought processes. Different Indian texts approach the issue differently, but a common notion is that of dharma.

Dharma is a difficult concept to understand because it is used in various senses in different contexts. Sometimes it stands for the right code of conduct, other times for duty and sometimes for religious injunctions. Generally, it does point to the way to lead an ethical life, and there are discourses in different ancient texts seeking to give advice on the right way to lead life. The *Ramayana* deals with the importance of doing your duty in an ideal manner, and in the *Yoga Vasishta*, Lord Rama is given a lengthy discourse on numerous aspects of life including ethical aspects by the sage Vasishta. Bhishma gives a similar discourse to Yudhishtira in the *Shanti Parva* in the *Mahabharata*, though this deals more with the duties of a king. Different stories such as those of Harishchandra, Sravana, Nala–Damayanti, etc. highlight the right action to be taken in different situations, and the need to uphold dharma even in trying circumstances. They generally take a clear stand on what is right and what is wrong. For example, Harishchandra and his wife went through incredible hardships in trying to uphold his word and his stand for truth. Sravana's life tells us about the supreme importance of serving others. Significantly, Mahatma Gandhi says, in his autobiography *My Experiments with Truth* (1927), that his values and concepts on how he should lead his life were deeply influenced by such stories.

But what may appear to be categorical imperatives become highly ambiguous and context dependent, as is repeatedly highlighted in the *Mahabharata*. The whole story deals with the complex nature of ethics and life, and gives no clear, unambiguous answers. Indeed, it seems to tell you that you cannot ask life what it means and what is right; it is life which keeps asking you constantly what you think is ethical and right and why.

The whole dilemma is best expressed by Bhishma when asked in the court by Draupadi after her dishonour as to what his dharma was in this episode. Bhishma's reply was, 'Draupadi, dharma is *sukshma*' (Das 2009). This word cannot really be translated into English; it roughly means that it is subtle, with many dimensions, and difficult to express clearly and concisely.

That is the real problem of understanding business ethics. They are all real problems that are, to quote Bhishma, sukshma. But they are problems that will not go away by just saying that they are sukshma, just as they did not go away in the *Mahabharata*. You need to confront them and develop better solutions in specific situations. This is what I shall do in the ensuing chapters.

CONCLUSION

In this chapter, I reviewed three major theories of ethics or rather approaches to ethical situations. I suggested that ethical issues need to be reflected upon and a conclusion arrived at. It is different from saying 'because I say so' or 'because this is my feeling'. The approaches will enable you to analyse a situation from different perspectives, weigh their pros and cons, and arrive at a decision. Different perspectives may lead to different conclusions, and then you have to reconcile them or choose among them. This involves a reflection on the questions, 'Who am I? What do I stand for?'

This is not as easy as it sounds for, when young, you in fact do not know who you are. Even over a period, you develop maturity and a consistency of attitudes and beliefs slowly. This process of development is the development of character.

I shall deal with these issues in more detail in Chapters 9 and 10. At this point, I note that resolving problems of any ethics is an entirely personal affair, that there can never be a 'final' answer, and, whatever you do, you could be questioned on ethical grounds. The answer to this problem, again, lies in reflection and development of your own point of view, a point of view that is all your own.

One distinguishing feature of business ethics, as distinct from personal ethics, is that in business, you are not taking decisions only about yourself (unless you are the sole owner of that business). You are acting as an agent and trustee of a variety of stakeholders, and what you do affects not only you but others as well. You have to deal with multiple stakeholders and reconcile their points of view as best as you can. This is the subject of the discussion in the next chapter.

KEY TAKEAWAYS

1. It is possible to reason, up to a point, the ethics of a decision.

2. There are multiple approaches that need to be utilized. They may lead to different conclusions. Again, you need to apply your value systems to make a choice.

3. No matter what approach you take, ethical decisions are not like engineering problems where some formulae can be applied. The context is always important.

4. Appreciation of how to apply the principles in a context can be done only by reflection and development of your personality and character.

REFERENCES

Camus, A. 1942. *L'Etranger*. Trans. J. Laredo, UK: Penguin Books.

'The Case of the Dying Fish', Case #BP 143. Ahmedabad: Indian Institute of Management, Ahmedabad.

Donaldson, T. and P.H. Werhane (eds). 1983. *Ethical Issues in Business: A Philosophical Approach*. Englewoods Cliffs, NJ: Prentice Hall.

Das, G. 2009. *The Difficulty of Being Good: On the Subtle Art of Dharma*. New Delhi: Allen Lane/Penguin Books India.

Gandhi, M.K. 1927. *An Autobiography or the Story of My Experiments with Truth*. Ahmedabad: Navjeevan Trust.

Hauser, M. 2006. *Moral Minds: How Nature Designed Our Universal Sense of Right and Wrong*. New York: HarperCollins.

Kotchian, C. 1977. 'The Payoff: Lockheed's 70 Day Mission to Tokyo', *Saturday Review*, pp. 7–12. July 9.

3

Between Scylla and Charibdys

'Is there no way of escaping Charybdis, and at the same time keeping Scylla off?', asked Odysseus.

—Homer, The Odyssey

There is the ancient Greek story about how, while returning from the Trojan War, in the sea between Italy and Sicily, Odysseus had to confront and choose between Scylla, a six-headed rock monster that would eat up the sailors passing near it, and Charybdis, a huge whirlpool. It was not possible to avoid both.

This is the kind of dilemma managers face, especially so in ethical situations. You cannot avoid the unpleasant alternatives and sidestep the issues; you have to take a stand and face the consequences.

Actually, Odysseus' problem was not half as difficult as is confronted by managers. He reasoned that by going close to Scylla he would lose only six of his men, while if he went near Charybdis he would lose the entire ship, and so chose Scylla.

A much starker choice is presented to Sophie in William Styron's novel *Sophie's Choice* (1979). She, along with her two children Eva and Jan, is taken to a Nazi concentration camp. At the entry, the sadist commandant of the camp tells her that he will not kill both the children but she must choose the one which will go to the gas chamber; the other will be sent to the children's camp. The choice is all hers, he adds cheerfully. If she does not choose, both will be sent to the gas chamber.

Sophie, after pleading with the commandant not to have her make that choice (to no avail), ultimately chooses to send her daughter Eva to death and saves her younger son, Jan, who is sent to the children's camp and whom she never meets again. Sophie herself spends time in the concentration camp, is released at the end of the war, goes to America and tries to build a new life. But guilt is constantly upon her; she cannot get rid of it. Eventually she kills herself.

Similarly, the kinds of choices managers need to make are between competing demands between competing stakeholders. Each of them has a case, yet the manager cannot satisfy them all. No matter what you do, you would be criticized. This is the nature of ethical dilemmas.

In this chapter, I set the broad contours of the nature of these dilemmas and choices. Notably, the choices are between the demands of the shareholders versus those of different stakeholders, customers, employees, the community the firm is located in, and the larger society. In the subsequent chapters, I shall look upon the ethical issues involved with each of these stakeholders separately; in this chapter, I shall briefly look at the nature of these conflicts and tradeoffs to give you a flavour of the nature of contradictions managers need to resolve.

SHAREHOLDERS: ONE OF THE STAKEHOLDERS OR THE ONLY STAKEHOLDER GROUP?

In Chapters 1 and 2, I briefly touched upon the viewpoint of the so-called Chicago School, spearheaded by Milton Friedman, that the *only* responsibility of a corporation is to its shareholders. This has been elaborated into the so-called Agency Theory, which will be discussed in Chapter 8. Briefly, this theory argues that shareholders 'own' the enterprise and they have appointed the manager to act on their behalf, with a mandate to maximize their returns. Thus the owners are the 'principals' and the managers their 'agents'. The duty of the managers is to carry out the wishes of the principals, whatever their personal views and preferences may be. Their *sole* job is to maximize shareholder value.

This approach has been taken further to argue that while managers have to act within the law, there is no place for any *ethical issues*. The corporation has no business looking at the morality of an issue and need not concern itself with the consequences of its actions to anyone other than the shareholders, so long as it makes its profits. A corporation is neither moral nor immoral, but an *amoral* entity. In other words, there is no such thing as business ethics, and there is no place for ethics in business.

This is not a view shared (fortunately) by many other scholars, or by practitioners. Somehow, it does not seem right to most of us. The opponents of this view argue that while shareholders might have contributed capital, others have also contributed various factors of production such as labour, knowledge, and goodwill, which go into the making of the final products or services the firm delivers. Peter Drucker, in his book *The Practice of Management* (1965), while arguing that the firm is primarily an economic entity and the economic duties of its managers come first, also argues that they are not the only duties. In fact, he goes to the extent of saying that the argument that the objective of the firm is to make profits is 'not only false, but it is irrelevant'. James C. Collins and Jerry I. Porras, in their book *Built to Last: Successful Habits of Visionary Companies* (1994) say that visionary companies—all of which studied by them had done exceptionally well in the stock market also—go beyond profits and strike an 'and' proposition: profits *and* core ideology, purpose *and* vision. Thus the firm is seen working *with* stakeholders rather than working *for* shareholders alone.

This necessarily involves tradeoffs among the demands posed by these different stakeholders. In the following chapters, I explore the ethical issues involved in dealing with the different stakeholders: community, society, buyers, employees, and so on. In this chapter, I shall attempt to give a flavour of the conflicts and contradictions involved in dealing with these stakeholders vis-à-vis the shareholders. I come back to the theme that business ethics is not about pure ethics as such, but is about resolving these conflicting demands and finding the best possible solution in each case.

SHAREHOLDERS VERSUS CUSTOMERS

Drucker wrote that 'There is only one valid definition of business purpose: to create a customer.' Thus every business ultimately exists for the sake of the customer. It is the customer who makes a business possible. Yet there is a conflict between what a customer wants from a firm and what a firm wants from a customer. While the customer wants the best product at the lowest price possible, the firm wants precisely the opposite. These interests are balanced at the point where both are, in some sense, satisfied. The firm's duty is to give the customer not what he wants but what is promised. The customer can choose to buy the product or ignore it. Here lies an ethical dilemma vis-à-vis the customer: Most transactions take place on an implicit rather than an explicit promise, and it is possible to shortchange a customer. If the firm does this in a sufficiently subtle way, is it doing its duty towards its shareholders? Should it pursue what it can get away with, what can be proved in a court of law and what cannot?

Similarly, there are issues with quality. Quality comes at a cost, and can be shortchanged. Is there a tradeoff here? If a firm adulterates, does not disclose the contents or the side effects of a drug, or cuts down on safety features without being technically illegal, is it really working in the best interests of its shareholders?

There are also issues regarding advertising. Should a firm enhance shareholders' profits by false and deceitful advertising that can just escape the law but is clearly designed to mislead? Should a firm enhance shareholder value by creating demand for harmful products?

What if a firm is in a monopolistic or quasi-monopolistic situation as, for example, Intel and Microsoft, with their dominant market shares? Should the firm use its monopoly power to make extraordinary profits? (It may be recalled that Microsoft has been the subject of many investigations, both in the USA and Europe.) What about pharmaceutical companies with their proprietary drugs for major diseases? They need to recover their investments in drug discovery and testing but once this is over, in many cases, such firms may have a near-monopoly position. Should they ignore patients' interests and concentrate on exploiting their monopoly powers for their shareholders?

The Chicago School would probably respond that everything is permissible so long as it is not illegal, or cannot be *proved to be illegal*. Judging from this standard, all the sub-prime lending, securitization, and other novel ways of disguising the nature of financial products might have been perfectly legal but few would agree that it is all perfectly fine.

It may also be argued that the firm should maximize *long-term* value for the shareholders and that shortchanging or misleading customers may pay in the short run, but in the *long run* the customers may defect and the shareholders would suffer erosion in value. This may indeed happen, but it may also be possible to carry on these practices for a remarkably long time before customer backlash happens.

More important, there is a distinction between economic tradeoffs and ethical tradeoffs. The former involves finding a point where the costs outweigh the benefits: finding the quality level at which a firm can best serve the customer at a given price. No one expects a low-cost airline to provide champagne, or, for that matter, free meals in-flight. Not doing so is not poor-quality service. The firm has decided and made it known that for the low price customers pay there are some services it can give, but these it will do well, as, for example, punctual running of the services; but there are some services that it will not give, and the customers should not expect them. The firm has made a tradeoff and put it upfront for customers to see, and some low-cost airlines have been successful and profitable, as, for example, India's Indigo. Ethical tradeoffs are different: An airline may not refund the fares when its flights are unduly delayed, overbooks and refuses boarding for passengers with valid reservations without offering compensation, or serves unhygienic or bad food on board knowing well that the passengers may not have much of an alternative, or demands additional charges at the last minute.

Ethical tradeoffs involve decisions on doing things that are *morally wrong*, knowing fully well that they are wrong, whatever be the legal position. Attracting customers through creative advertising that basically draws attention to the product and presents its best features is one thing; deliberately making misleading claims about a product is another. Pricing high upfront for a quality product is one thing; putting hidden charges and not disclosing them is quite another. The tradeoff consists in drawing the line and saying, 'Here is the line I draw. The shareholders may indeed profit (at least in the short term) more if I go beyond the line but my personal values and the values I seek to build in the organization do not permit me to do so.'

SHAREHOLDERS VERSUS EMPLOYEES

As in the case of customers, in the case of employees also there is an inherent conflict between the interests of employees and shareholders. Clearly, employees want the highest compensation possible, while taking care of the shareholders' interest would imply giving them the least to ensure that adequate manpower is available and is retained.

In the case of employees there is, in many cases, a more explicit contract, namely, the terms of employment. But often these are not honoured. This is a widely reported problem in cases of employment in the Gulf countries where, on landing, the person finds that the terms of employment are completely changed, and he cannot even refuse the job and return, since passports are usually impounded by the employer as soon as the prospective employee lands in the country. In India, contractors are reported to engage in the practice of underpayment widely. If the employees are unable to fight back, is it fine to pay them less than the contract with a view to maximizing the shareholders' value (for avoiding legal suits, their signatures may be forcibly obtained for the contract amount)? Is it permissible to coerce them into working beyond the terms of employment without payment (for example, overtime)?

Even die-hard supporters of the Chicago School may not support these ideas. Yet they follow directly from the Agency Theory.

Other issues that arise are: Should the employees' right to strike be respected? Should they be given the right of self-defence before punishment? How should firms deal with whistleblowers who seek to expose wrong practices of the company? Is there a conflict here as well with the interests of shareholders?

SHAREHOLDERS VERSUS COMMUNITY AND SOCIETY

Here conflicts between the shareholders and the 'outside stakeholders' become sharp. There are laws governing pollution, exploitation of resources, perhaps local employment, acquisition of land, and so on. These can vary from country to country and state to state; their enforcement may be slack or rigorous. Much deforestation, quarrying, and mining are carried out with the connivance of government officials, a connivance for which they are well paid. It is not easy to 'prove' these cases, especially in India where investigation is weak, incompetent, and generally corrupt. Should companies take advantage of these weaknesses in the system and work for enhancing shareholders' value?

Two questions arise while relating a firm to the community and society: Are there any obligations or desirable actions a firm should carry out *beyond* the legal requirements, and if it does, is it acting against shareholder interests? Is it ethically permissible for a firm to exploit loopholes in the law or its weak enforcement so as to maximize returns to its shareholders?

As I will show in Chapters 7 and 8, the answers are not straightforward; there are several conflict situations in which a firm needs to take a call. For example, even if the pollution created by a company is within the legal norms, if it seriously affects the livelihood of the members of the community near the plant, should it install additional pollution control measures (and get less profit)? This was the dilemma faced by Zuari Agrochemicals (see Chapter 2). If there is an industry accident and a large number of people are killed or their health affected, should the company be responsible for the damages or should it take shelter under protracted legal proceedings? This is the question I shall discuss in Chapter 8, taking the Bhopal tragedy as an example. If there are no enforceable norms or the action cannot be quantified, is it permissible to draw underground water in an arid region, leading to water shortage in the nearby villages? This was the case with Coca-Cola India in the village of Plachimada in Kerala (see Chapter 1).

There is also the issue of corporate social responsibility (CSR). Are such activities to be undertaken at all? Many firms do undertake such activities, and I shall give examples of such activities in Chapter 8. Ultimately the firm is using the money of the shareholders for what clearly are not the core activities of the organization. Even though it may be claimed that it will improve its image in the longer run and that will be beneficial to the shareholders, this connection is difficult to establish. So are firms actually *unethical* in using the shareholders' money in such initiatives? If they do use some money for such purposes, what amount is 'reasonable' and why?

Do the actions of business organizations affect societal attitudes and values? Should a corporation worry about it? Can a firm sell dangerous, unsafe, or harmful goods to increase shareholder value? Should it issue advertisements that persuade consumers to take up bad habits (such as smoking) or shape their attitudes towards ethnic groups, castes, or women? Is there some point of balance between the shareholders' interests (at least in the short run)?

Many such questions arise, and the common theme is that it is not possible to take an extreme view in any of the cases. Managers will need to take a stand on every issue and go beyond the legal requirements. This book assumes that 'anything goes so long as you don't get caught' (the so called eleventh commandment: Thou can do all the above, but thou shalt not get caught), is not an attitude firms can, or rather, should take. Ethics are needed to project an image of the firm, build a certain type of relationship with its stakeholders, and balance its duty towards its shareholders with other considerations.

The following chapters examine the issues involved in dealing with each of the above stakeholders, see the tradeoffs involved, and leave you with the responsibility to decide where you want to be, what you want to do.

KEY TAKEAWAYS

1. Ethical issues are not just a simple matter of saying whether the acts are ethical or unethical. The managers have to choose between different actions, each of which has their right and wrong aspects.

2. The old notion that shareholders are the only constituency that needs to be addressed is not held by most managers today. Hence, a more useful notion would be considering stakeholders rather than shareholders.

3. Managers face conflicts between different groups of stakeholders: between shareholders and customers; shareholders and employees; shareholders, community and society, and also among the non-shareholder groups themselves. Managers need to resolve these conflicts.

REFERENCES

Collins, J. C. and J. I. Porras (eds). 1994. *Built to Last: Successful Habits of Visionary Companies*. London: Random House Business Books.

Drucker, P. 1965. *The Practice of Management*. London: Mercury Books.

Styron, W. 1979. *Sophie's Choice*. New York: Random House.

4

Caveat Emptor!

'The most significant clause in our trading charter is the promise to integrate principles with profits. It gives other people the spotlight and keeps achievement in a healthy perspective.'

—Anita Roddick, Founder, The Body Shop

In this chapter, I examine the ethical issues that arise in corporations while dealing with customers. I had earlier drawn a distinction between legal issues and ethical issues, and had argued that what is legal need not be ethical. Here I am not so much concerned with what corporations have to do to satisfy legal requirements, as what is needed if their dealings with customers are to be seen as *ethical*. But I will first look briefly at the legal requirements of corporation–customer relationships before going on to explore the ethical issues.

CAVEAT EMPTOR: BUYER, BEWARE!

This was the credo in the early days of capitalism. The buyer was expected to look at a product to his satisfaction before buying it; but once he had bought it, the responsibility of the seller ceased. This is not such an outdated credo as it looks at first sight: most second-hand sales, as, for example, of cars or television sets, are done on an 'as-is-where-is' basis, which basically works on the above principle. It is understood that in such deals, except in exceptional circumstances, the deal once closed is closed, period.

But this is not the way corporations have to function today. They have certain duties towards their customers. Broadly, these are: to be truthful about the product/service offered and its features; the price to be charged; what to do in the case of a defective product; and not to coerce a buyer into buying a product.

Then there are issues arising from the above, but these need separate treatment: truthfulness in advertising, misleading advertisements, and promotion practices. Here, besides corporations, advertising agencies are also involved.

RELATIONSHIP BETWEEN A CORPORATION AND A BUYER

It is the generally accepted view today that buying constitutes a contract between the buyer and seller, even though no contract might have been formally entered into. The sales transactions are governed by the Contract Act and the Sale of Goods Act, and a seller cannot get away with saying that there is no written contract with the buyer.

A contract implies the fulfillment of certain obligations by both the parties. The buyer's obligations are, of course, to pay, and use the product with due prudence and diligence. If any operating instructions are given, the buyer needs to adhere to them. Much of the seller's obligations are *implied*: the product must be what it is purported to be, and do what it is meant to do; it must be free from defects; it should not cause any harm to the buyer; if it carries any risks, these need to be disclosed; if the product does have a defect, suitable rectification needs to be carried out, and so on. Because certain terms are implied rather than explicit, at times there is scope for difference in their interpretation.

The Indian Railways had to confront many issues at different times. In the old days, it had always taken a position that it was just a carrier and the amenities provided were, so to speak, *gratis*, including water, lights, and fans. There were some instances when the window shutters (in the old types of coaches) that needed to be lifted *up* and latched did not get secured properly, fell down and caused injuries to the fingers of the person sitting next to the window. The Railways denied any liabilities for such injuries, but the courts consistently held it liable. Today, issues of responsibility and compensation in case of accidents, and for robberies and crimes in running trains are being addressed and the responsibility is placed on the Railways. Recently there was the case of Arunima, a national volleyball player who was pushed out of a train by some chain snatchers, and lost her legs. The Railways gave an ex-gratia payment immediately but declared (with justification) that it was simply not possible to police every compartment in every train. While not invalidating the argument, the court still ordered the Railways to compensate her for a much larger sum. Similarly, in cases of frauds, banks are held responsible in many cases.

If suitable and comprehensive instructions on how to use a product are not given, the seller is held liable. Thus assembly instructions for, say, a mixer grinder need to be clearly given, as also the precautions needed to be taken so that the blades do not fly out and injure the person operating it.

These are legal requirements. Now I will look, in some more detail, at the ethical obligations of sellers vis-à-vis buyers, beyond the legal requirements.

DUTY TO DISCLOSE THE FEATURES
OF A PRODUCT

Part of this disclosure comes through advertising but part of it also comes from company brochures, what the company sales personnel tell the customers, and certain features that are assumed. Their purpose should be to inform, not to conceal.

In the case of pharmaceuticals, for example, this implies a full disclosure of what the product will do or will not do, and the possible side effects it may have. A special problem with pharmaceuticals is that they are purchased on the advice of doctors, and it is a tricky question as to what kind of information should be put on the packaging for the benefit of the patient. Usually, companies put some information on the product packaging but this is rarely read or understood by a typical patient. The doctor has also the obligation, as a part of his medical service, to convey this information to the patient fully.

A recent example of serious non-disclosure of a product that has come into focus is insurance products, specifically, Unit Linked Insurance Products (ULIPs) sold (or mis-sold) by insurance companies (see Box 4.1). With these products, there was rampant mis-selling by insurance agents who were paid attractive incentives to sell these products. There were many complaints from customers about the selling practices of these agents, and the result has been recent tightening of the rules by the regulatory authorities. Despite this, ULIPs are still viewed with some mistrust by consumers, making it difficult for the companies to sell them, even if they are well designed.

ULIPs (Unit-linked insurance products) are part insurance, part market investments based on equity. Insurance companies used to charge large upfront charges, often as high as 25 percent of one year's premium, sometimes even more, and the consumers were rarely informed. The insurance component varied with the policies but there were even policies that had no insurance component at all (yet carried large upfront charges). It was very difficult to get out of these policies since the terms of surrender were kept extremely adverse.

Based on numerous customer complaints, the regulatory authorities have tightened the terms under which these policies can be issued. In the meantime, ULIPs have acquired a bad image.

Financial products are generally complex, and the consumer needs to be informed of all the aspects of a product. Yet this is rarely done; on the other hand, financial companies give such incentives to their agents that actually encourage them to suppress vital information (such as hidden charges). Often agents induce the customers to surrender older policies and take fresh ones, with an eye on the incentives they could get. With reference to the ULIPs, full information was rarely given even in the brochures, but was usually given only in the policy, and usually in long-winded legal language that most would find hard to disentangle. Many customers discovered the real terms of a policy only after they actually received it, or tried to surrender or discontinue the payment of premium.

Such deliberate non-disclosure violates all the ethical approaches I discussed in Chapter 2. Kant would definitely classify such practices as unethical, since they restrict the free choice of customers and do not recognize their right to be fully informed. From a utilitarian point of view, such behaviour leads to disutility for a vast number of people to benefit a few, and even the firms themselves stand to lose in the long run, since they invite a regulatory backlash and loss of trust from customers.

What Should You, as an Ethical Manager, Do?

You need to fully disclose all the features of the product and ensure that the customers understand them. Deliberate misrepresentation is, of course, unethical beyond question, but subtle disguising and distortions, while they can pass the legal test, would fail to pass the ethical test.

PRICING

In a free and competitive market, pricing is supposed to be decided by the market. But markets are not necessarily free or competitive in many cases. Monopolies are examples where the market mechanism breaks down. This can be extended to quasi-monopolies or firms having a dominant market share. Setting a monopoly price is usually not illegal but besides the ethical aspects, extortionate pricing by monopolies attracts regulatory attention.

Microsoft has a hugely dominant share of the market for operating systems of computers and core applications (such as word processing, spreadsheets, etc.). The company is immensely profitable, and naturally it was bound to attract adverse criticism. It has been subject to lawsuits regarding alleged monopolistic practices (such as clubbing its search engine, Internet Explorer

(IE), and Windows Media Player with its operating systems, the Windows X versions), its attack on Netscape leading to its eventual winding up, and so on. Courts have debated on Microsoft being broken up, similar to the way the telephone giant AT&T was broken up into Baby Bells. Such scrutiny has arisen from a perception that dominant companies have not acted ethically or fairly in pricing and in dealing with competition.

BOX 4.2

The Legal Battles of Microsoft

The software giant Microsoft has been engaged in legal battles during most of its existence, many being lawsuits and investigations against its pricing and bundling practices. In 2004, a class action suit accused Microsoft of overcharging its customers, and Microsoft settled the case for a sum of $1.1 billion, plus legal costs of $258 million. It went into major litigation in the USA and the EU regarding the bundling of its browser with the operating system. Microsoft argued that this bundling was the result of innovation, and the browser had been tightly linked to the operating system so that it was not possible to separate the two. It went on to argue that the customers were getting the benefits of its IE for free. The customers ended up having IE on their computers, whether they wanted it or not; they had to pay separately for another browser, which most would not like to do. This stifled competition from browsers such as Netscape and Opera.

The anti-trust case initiated by the EU was much more damaging to Microsoft. This started in 2003–4, affecting the business of other European media player developers. It was fined $497

---

million, and Microsoft was required to ship Windows without the Media Player and supply the protocols needed for Windows capability to other developers. In 2007 the case was revived, alleging that Microsoft was not giving the needed information. The judgment was against Microsoft; it appealed and lost. Eventually it paid a fine of over $1.3 billion on this case, and about $2.5 billion for many other cases it was involved in. Most of these cases were basically about abuse of its monopoly position.

Source: http://en.wikipedia.org/wiki/Microsoft_litigation, accessed on June 10, 2011.

Pharmaceutical companies are also subject to constant scrutiny. These companies are highly profitable, allegedly because of their monopoly power with regard to lifesaving medicines for particular diseases such as tuberculosis and for cancer treatment. Due to a perception of unfair pricing (it rarely escapes the attention of people that pharma companies seem to do very well financially), price regulation and control are exerted even in a free country like the USA through many devices.

Another problem is the collusion in pricing between the majors in an industry. There are legal safeguards such as anti-trust regulation, but collusion is notoriously difficult to prove. Yet when companies indulge in such unethical behaviour, it is not long before it gets noticed and public pressure is exerted on them.

When prices for a product or service are to be recovered over a period of time, the *pricing pattern* also becomes important. The so-called teaser rates for home loans fall under this category. The idea is to offer a low interest rate in the early years and ramp it up in subsequent years. There is nothing unethical as such in this arrangement, and indeed it may go in tandem with the earning capacities of the borrowers that may increase over a period of time. The problem comes with the way the customer is explained these loans, and after a few years, when the interest rates go up, the needed payments go beyond the capacity of the borrowers, and defaults ensue. This is more or less what happened in the notorious sub-prime crisis of 2008–9. Some of the recent problems faced by microfinance companies also arise from their high interest rates, combined with aggressive lending and questionable recovery practices.

BOX 4.3

Lending to Sub-prime Borrowers

It has been widely acknowledged that the financial crisis and the recession of 2008–9 were caused by extensive 'sub-prime' lending resorted to by banks, especially in the USA. Sub-prime lending refers to lending to people who may have difficulty in repayment due to their financial position and earning potential. These are people who otherwise would have no access to credit.

Banks found the people not only worth lending to, but also highly profitable (at least on paper). To avoid high initial mortgage payments, mainly for houses, the loans were given with adjustable rate mortgages (ARMs), basically with low interest rates in the beginning, and increasing steadily. Annual adjustments could be around 2 percent or more per year. These rates were not always fixed, but linked to the prevalent interest rates. Many borrowers were neither explained properly the way the repayments would work, nor did the banks take a realistic look at the capacity of their borrowers for repayment later on. Soon many borrowers found it difficult to repay the higher installments and started defaulting. Rising interest rates added to the problems. The mortgaged houses could, in theory, be taken back by banks and

---

What Should You, as an Ethical Manager, Do?

You need to go not strictly by the rule of what the market can bear, but by considering what is a fair price, and whether the consumers targeted can actually afford that price.

DEALING WITH A DEFECTIVE PRODUCT/SERVICE

It is the duty of a manufacturer or service provider to ensure that the product/service delivers what it purports to deliver. If it fails to do so, there are legal obligations to repair or replace the product and/or offer suitable compensation. Such obligations are covered under warranty clauses.

Ethical issues arise in the way warranty claims are actually dealt with, the disclaimers that cover a wide variety of contingencies, and in drawing up the warranty clauses in such a manner that the document is outright incomprehensible to the consumer, and difficult or costly to enforce. An easy way to do this is to hold the warranty null and void if the user has not used the product with 'due care': whether the user has exercised due care would be decided at 'the sole discretion of the manufacturer'. Another way is to require the customer to ship back the defective product to the manufacturer at the user's expense, which the manufacturer very well knows will exceed the possible warranty benefits the consumer might get under a variety of circumstances.

A particularly important case is when the defective product leads to heavy consequential damages, or to loss of life or limbs. This was the case with the famous case of Ford Pinto (see Box 4.4). Here the car manufacturer, Ford Motor Company, knew that in their new design the petrol tank was positioned at the rear of the vehicle, increasing the risk of fire in case of a collision from behind. Matters became worse when it came to light that the company had calculated the chances of such collisions, the possible damages to be paid and the cost savings realized by the new design. This was interpreted as the company's indifference to human life and treating people as merely statistics in an economic calculation.

BOX 4.4

The Case of Ford Pinto

The Ford Pinto was a small car designed and launched in the early 1970s to compete with the Volkswagen. It had a rear petrol tank located near the bumper, making it vulnerable to fire hazards in the event of a rear collision. It was alleged (later in lawsuits against the firm) that Ford engineers knew about this risk, but due to competition from Volkswagen, the car was pushed out in a hurry. According to Mark Dowie, General Manager, *Mother Jones* magazine business operations, the Pinto's crashes were indeed hazardous and had caused more than 500 deaths by burns, and by 1977, perhaps as many as 900.

In the late 1960s, new safety standards were attempted to be laid down, among them Standard 301, which mandated that cars needed to withstand crashes at speeds of up to 20 mph. Pinto cars could not pass this test in case of rear end collisions. But the tooling and machinery were in place to produce the Pinto,

---

and the company did not want to delay its launch. So, it was alleged, Ford lobbied hard to prevent Standard 301 legislation from materializing.

A modification costing $11 per car could have substantially, if not totally, prevented the rupture of fuel tanks in case of collision. This was not adopted by the company, based on a cost–benefit analysis. The company calculated the costs (at $11 per car) versus the cost per death and injury ($200,000 per death, $67,000 for injury, and $700 per vehicle), and decided that the costs of provision of safety features ($137 million) far outweighed the costs of death and injury ($49.5 million), assuming 180 burn deaths and 180 serious burn injuries. This calculation, when it became public, resulted in a hue and cry and the company was accused of being callous with human lives. For some reason, the company did not give the modification as an optional extra.

Ford paid millions of dollars for out-of-court settlements, and far more for lobbying against the new standards (which did come into effect in 1977). For the first time, the *company* (not its executives) was charged with culpable homicide, following a crash in 1978. When the Pinto was hit from behind, it burst into flames, killing two teenage girls inside it. Though the company was found not guilty, the charge dented its image badly.

It was made out in the trial that most of the car accidents Pinto cars were involved in were major accidents involving high-speed collision, in which the victims had no chance anyway. All the same, the Pinto case reinforced the image of corporations as amoral and callous entities. It also came out during the trials that Ford was not the only company doing such cost–benefit calculations. Lobbying against inconvenient legislation, needless to say, has been a feature in the US landscape then and now.

Source: Michael Hoffman, 'The Ford Pinto', in Michael Hoffman and Jennifer Mills Moore (eds), *Business Ethics*, New York: McGraw Hill, 1984.

What Should You, as an Ethical Manager, Do?

You need to have clear and fair policies regarding defective products and services. It should be possible for consumers to actually use the redress mechanism regarding their complaints. Special care needs to be taken regarding the safety of the product.

ETHICS IN ADVERTISING

There are major differences in opinions over fundamental issues regarding advertising itself, such as whether advertising merely raises the costs and the eventual price to the consumer, whether it creates desire in the mind of the consumer, not always in the right direction, and whether it is inherently deceptive. These are concerns regarding the ethics *of* advertising.

Then there are issues regarding the ethics *in* advertising, that is, what kinds of norms should be observed in advertising. These consist of topics such as truthfulness (or at least not intentional misleading) in advertising, avoidance of obscene or offensive materials, deliberate maligning of competitors, and appreciation of the impact on young and impressionable minds. Promotion also, at times, involves such ethical issues.

I shall focus on ethics *in* advertising rather than on ethics *of* advertising, which is essentially a philosophical issue.

Truthfulness in Advertising

When asked to justify advertising, firms have argued that advertisements carry information about the product and what it does. Though this may be true in many cases (here I am referring to commercial advertisements and not those such as notifications which are indeed nothing but dissemination of information), it is not true in many others. Certainly, even if *some* information is conveyed, clearly the purpose of advertising is not so much information dissemination as persuading a prospective buyer into buying the product.

This means that to persuade prospective buyers is to extol the virtues of the product, describe what it can accomplish (often with some exaggeration), and 'position' the product in the minds of consumers by association with another experience or benefit. Thus a car may create an image of being well engineered, having exclusive safety features, comfort, luxuriousness, and so on. A particular brand of perfume may be positioned as enhancing sex appeal, a soap brand as enhancing complexion, a hair oil brand as helping hair to grow thick and luxurious, and so on.

The main ethical issue is one of truthfulness of the claims made, if any. Saying Coca-Cola is the real thing or Heineken is a great beer is not saying anything specific, and no issue of truthfulness is involved. But if a manufacturer claims that a fairness cream makes its users fairer in complexion while it does nothing of the sort, or bleaches the skin causing other damages, then that is something else. Then there are health drinks that claim make a young boy tough and muscular, or even add height, while there may be absolutely no evidence of any such effects. Clearly, a wrong and untruthful message is conveyed deliberately.

If messages are outright false, companies go beyond the purview of ethics, and they are likely to be sued and held liable. Though such suits are common in Western countries, especially in the USA, with increased activism and some activity by consumer courts (meagre though this may be), such legal actions are becoming more common in India as well. But companies resort to more subtle devices to stay (just) short of the legal line, with the clear intention to mislead. For example, many over-the-counter (OTC) drugs, toothpastes, mouthwashes, etc. are 'recommended' by a person wearing white overalls, and perhaps with a stethoscope on his person, the clear intention being to mislead the audience into thinking that the person making such a recommendation is a doctor, and that his claims have medical support. Of course anyone can wear white overalls and put a stethoscope around his neck, and as such no *outright* falsehood is involved. Thus while the advertisement may not be legally challengeable, having the clear intention to create a wrong impression violates ethical standards.

Even though such intentional misleading will definitely go against Kant's notion of categorical imperative ('deception is not to be encouraged'), supporters of such advertisements may justify such deception on a relativistic argument that in such a context, no one *expects the advertisement to be fully truthful*. But from an ethics perspective, this cannot be supported since it is not known who or how many get deceived and in what manner. Thus you may buy a hair dye based on its claim of making your hair a lustrous black, but find that it leads to other side effects such as loss of hair. From a consequentialist perspective, the overall utility is not increased since the product has not delivered any tangible benefit despite the costs incurred in advertising.

What Should You, as an Ethical Manager, Do?

You need to present a fair picture of the product or service, and what it can or cannot do. Intentional misleading, however subtle it may be, definitely goes against the canons of ethics.

Avoidance of Offensive and Indecent Materials

What is offensive and indecent or obscene is always a tricky affair, and as society evolves, norms change: That which was considered obscene fifty years back may be perfectly fine now. For example, nudity in advertisements is generally considered offensive, but may be acceptable, if tastefully done, in particular societies. All the same, generally speaking, advertisements should not offend the sensibilities of the majority of any society, whether they conform to the obscenity laws or not. Surely, putting the image of Gandhi on shoes may be considered highly offensive in India (and in some other countries).

Objection to fairness creams comes from their glorification of fair skin, presenting it as more desirable and dark skin as less so. Similarly, advertisements poking fun at a particular community or ethnic group could be offensive to that group, and the fact that a vastly larger majority might actually enjoy them does not make them acceptable (for example, the 'Sardarji' jokes in India).

Gender is a sensitive issue today, and advertising that portrays women in the stereotypes of being submissive, sacrificing for their families, less intelligent, or incapable of taking decisions are today definitely not likely to pass the test of conformance to ethical standards.

Legal standards are present but evidently a call needs to be taken by managers as to the standards they set for themselves.

Advertisements are essentially a creative effort and are meant to attract attention hence often different approaches are tried. What passes for a harmless joke may in fact get much adverse attention. It is difficult to specify a rigid set of 'dos' and 'don'ts' but managers need to be sensitive to how an audience reacts to an advertisement.

BOX 4.5

Skin Lightening Creams

Hindustan Unilever's Fair and Lovely is the leading skin lightening cream for women in India. In 2004, it ran a series of advertisements depicting depressed, dark-complexioned women who had been ignored by employers and men. After using the skin lightening cream (and emerging much fairer than before), they found new boyfriends and careers. After an outcry, the company was forced to withdraw its advertisements in 2007.

Source: http:/en.wikipedia.org/wiki/Hindustan_unilever, accessed on June 11, 2011.

In 2003, Hindustan Unilever aired a television advertisement showing a dark-skinned young girl's father bemoaning his fate of not having a son and the (dark-skinned) girl not earning enough. The girl uses the skin lightening cream, becomes fairer, gets a job as an air hostess, and makes her father happy. There was a row over this advertisement as well: it was called a 'highly racist' campaign, 'equating fairness with beauty' and 'demeaning women'. It was taken off air.

Source: http:/news.bbc.co.uk/2/hi/south-asia/3089495.stm, July 24, 2003, accessed on June 11, 2011.

What Should You, as an Ethical Manager, Do?

You should avoid offensive and obscene materials, and those that could cause distress to parts of the audience. Certain issues are becoming important today, as, for example, gender and racial issues.

Deliberate Maligning of Competitors

Deliberate maligning of competitors is usually illegal, and definitely unethical. It is one thing to project the unique qualities of your product, and another to claim superiority to other products unjustifiably. Some of these issues come under untruthfulness. For example, there are advertisements showing 'actual trials' with the product and another 'competitor's product' which, while not showing the name of the competitor's product, shows its packaging, etc. in such a way as to leave no doubt in the viewer's mind as to which the object of comparison is. Some advertisements are much more subtle, giving one point of comparison while ignoring others. For example, a health drink may emphasize its superior and unique taste while it may not be superior with regard to its core benefit, namely, its health-related properties.

Usually, companies try to be just on the right side of the legal line knowing very well that they are clearly on the wrong side of the ethical line. The intention remains, however, not to convey any real information about the product, or to convey partial, distorted, or downright untrue information, and to mislead the consumer with regard to the competitor's products, hiding under the dictum 'caveat emptor'!

What Should You, as an Ethical Manager, Do?

Avoid denigration or maligning of competitors. There are usually enough virtues in your own product, without denigrating others.

Awareness about Impact on Society

It has been found in studies that advertisements can impact minds in different ways, especially young and impressionable minds. Advertisements containing dangerous stunts may lead to children trying to imitate them and injuring themselves seriously or even fatally. At least in the relatively well-to-do sections of society children have an increasing say not only regarding the products they consume but also regarding those consumed by their parents, especially in the matter of toys, dress, food, vacations, etc. Promotion of junk food, especially when done with clever and appealing visuals, appeals to children, who demand such food incessantly. It has been alleged that in the US, which has become an obese society, carbonated drinks containing large calories, and foods such as burgers and pizzas have contributed to the obesity problem in children, as well as the consequent medical costs incurred. The effect of cigarette advertisements, showing healthy people with vigorous outdoor lifestyles, or showing smoking as the 'in' thing has been documented, and it has been found that such advertisements do promote smoking in young people, especially teenagers, as of course they are intended to do. Alcohol promotions tend to project a classy image of drinking and induce people to drink, often even leading to addiction. Even when alcohol advertisements are banned (as in India), surrogate advertisements ostensibly promoting mineral water or soda (often with the same name as the alcoholic drink) are resorted to, with little doubt about the real product being advertised.

There is no question that tobacco causes cancer, and smoking increases the chances of lung cancer drastically. Cigarette advertisements downplay this impact, and instead glorify smoking as a social lubricant. Even when there are regulations requiring explicit mention of the harmful effects of smoking on cigarette packets, these warnings are printed in ultra-small letters. The cigarette industry all over the world has been resisting sterner measures such as the inclusion of visuals of the impact on health in advertisements and even dissemination of such information by other activists is sought to be neutralized.

Here, the ethical issue is the deliberate creation of a need or desire through subtle manipulation of young minds. Besides the direct impact on the user so persuaded, there is also the larger impact on society such as increased health costs, loss of productivity, etc. (It is estimated that despite the much touted tax contributions by the cigarette industry, the health costs caused by smoking outweigh these benefits by many times.)

Such persuasion need not be confined to children. A particularly interesting case has been that of advertising and promotion of infant milk food by various manufacturers, especially Nestlé. This came in for sharp criticism from many activist groups. Box 4.6 gives an idea of the controversy. Briefly, the issue concerned the ethics of persuading mothers of newborn babies to switch to infant food, discontinuing breastfeeding very early. Box 4.6 shows how complicated the issue is, mixing up a genuine need (when the mother does not have adequate milk) to a subtle indication to abandon breastfeeding because of the 'superior' nutritional qualities of infant foods, promoted with images of chubby babies. Infant foods were promoted in the maternity wards of hospitals through paid nurses; giving free samples; and not adequately emphasizing the importance of the correct procedures for sterilization of the vessels, bottles, and nipples, and the quantity of infant food needed. This became one of the most famous cases regarding ethics in advertising and promotion.

BOX 4.6

The Infant Food Formula Controversy

Infant food formulas developed in the 1920s, were regularly used in the US thereafter. So the product itself was not the problem. These formulas gained a push in the 1960s when the birth rates in the Western countries, especially in the US, started declining. But in the late 1960s, the manufacturers of these products expanded their sales into third world countries. Five companies became major players: four American companies, namely, Bristol-Myers, Abbott Laboratories, American Home Products and Borden's, and one Swiss company, Nestlé. Borden's and Nestlé were food manufacturers while the other three were pharmaceutical companies. Nestlé was by far the largest player in this business, commanding a world market share of nearly 50 percent, with a strong hold in many third world countries.

In the early 1970s, health officials and researchers in third world countries noted that the incidence of malnutrition and diarrhoea was increasing after the introduction of these infant formulas. The problems were twofold: (a) although the product packaging clearly showed the amount needed per feed, the poorer mothers (many of whom could not read) had a tendency to dilute the formulation to save on the cost (the product was not very cheap); and (b) again, though the importance of sterilization of the bottles and nipples was clearly mentioned by the manufacturers, as also the importance of clean water, in reality it was difficult to ensure

---

both. Water available to poorer sections was of doubtful quality, and it would not be boiled adequately to make it safe for babies. Moreover, advertising was intense and ubiquitous in many countries, essentially conveying the message that these products led to better health in babies. Breastfeeding was never discouraged and many advertisements even mentioned the superiority of mother's milk, and did convey that the infant formulas could be used conveniently when mother's milk was deficient. But such messages tended to be in small letters, certainly not as large as those extolling the virtues of the product. In many countries maternity wards were full of large poster advertisements, inducing mothers to wean the babies quickly. Also drawing criticism was the promotion by these companies through nurses and even doctors who were paid commissions based on sales. There were also 'mother-craft' nurses employed by the companies to give 'advice' to mothers regarding nutrition to babies, and free booklets with titles such as *A Life Begins* and *Your Baby and You* were given out.

In the early and mid-1970s, there was much outcry about these practices. There were calls for boycotts of the products of these companies, especially those of Nestlé. Consequent to the adverse publicity, these companies published a so-called code which went some way in tackling the issues, but many critics were dissatisfied with the loopholes still left, especially the soft-peddling of advertising practices. Abbott Laboratories adopted a much more comprehensive code, including surveillance and enforcement of its codes by its staff. The companies argued that many third world mothers were poor and themselves malnourished and did not have the capacity to breastfeed their children. These children, they argued, would be worse off without the supplements available in the form of infant formulas. Their 'mother-crafting' nurses were in fact doing a service by advising the mothers on the need for a nourishing diet to the babies and other health related issues.

Manufacturers of infant formulas have become more sensitive about the issues and the issue lost steam from the 1980s onwards.

Source: Compiled from many sources, including http://en.wikipedia.org/wiki/Infant_formula, accessed on June 12, 2011.

Clearly, the issues are complex and it is difficult to prescribe unambiguously what is ethical in such matters. Cigarette advertisements pose much less of an ethical issue: Their intention is to persuade the young to take up smoking; many of them would get addicted. Here again, the issues become less clear-cut when considering the claim by cigarette companies that since people will smoke anyway, in the absence of any control on the beedi industry, cigarettes may in fact be doing a service, being much less harmful than beedis.

It has been argued that advertisements offer only a choice to the consumer, and it is up to the latter to make the choice. This assumes a level of being informed and the capability to make mature and dispassionate choices on the part of the audience. This, however, is not the case, and companies know it. It is amazing to what extent even well-educated people get influenced and persuaded by advertisements.

The ethical issue here is really about the nature and extent of persuasion employed by the company. Persuasion to purchase a product that is not in the larger interests of society as a whole is definitely not ethical, whatever may be its legal status. The same applies to turning a blind eye to harmful consequences, and put the onus on the consumer with the motto, 'caveat emptor'.

What Should You, as an Ethical Manager, Do?

You need to be sensitive about how your advertising and promotion practices impact society. Advertisements promoting violence, sexual misconduct, exploitation of the ignorance and vulnerability of sections of society, etc. need to be avoided. While it may be difficult to specify what will or will not impact society, certain themes are *known* to promote undesirable behaviours, and these should be avoided. Moreover, if it becomes known that the advertisements are producing undesirable effects, or are objected to by sizeable sections of society, they should be withdrawn.

CONCLUSION

In this chapter, I have attempted to highlight the ethical issues involved in dealing with consumers. The first is the ethical obligation to deliver the product or service that is supposed to be delivered. Whether there is an explicit contract with the consumer or not, there is an implied contract. With industrial products, this contract is much more explicit, but with consumer products, it is conveyed through advertisements and promotion literature. The second is to offer it at a reasonable price, not taking advantage of any possible monopoly position. Third, in case the product does have a problem, there is an obligation to make suitable amends.

In today's world, advertisements play a vital role in creating and sustaining demand for products. Ethics in advertising concerns the truthfulness of the content, standards regarding obscenity and offensiveness, not hurting the feelings of any group, and not maligning competitors. Creation of demand, especially in children and adolescents, is a sensitive issue—what kinds of demands are promoted and whether they are conducive to societal welfare.

Most companies recognize that ethical dealings with consumers benefit them in the long run, but the issues are complex and vary from case to case. When the competition is resorting to unethical practices, what is a company supposed to do: retaliate, or stick to its principles?

What this chapter has sought to do is to present the multiple aspects of the issues involved with consumers, rather than give clear, unambiguous answers. The issues are undoubtedly complex and need to be dealt with at multiple levels. The resolution will ultimately depend on the ethical standards of its decision makers.

KEY TAKEAWAYS

1. The old dictum 'caveat emptor' is not ethically acceptable. Companies are expected to discharge legal responsibilities which are coming under greater scrutiny. In addition, the ethical responsibilities are also coming under scrutiny.

2. First, there is the responsibility to let a customer know the features of the product the company is offering and ensure that the product given is the same as what was promised, whether expressly or implicitly.

3. Second, companies are expected to set prices fairly and not take advantage of any monopolistic advantage they may have, or, with a limited number of competitors, not to indulge in practices such as the formation of cartels.

4. Interestingly, setting a *low* price in the beginning so as to entice customers who actually do not have the capacity to make further payments (the so-called teaser rates) also may not be ethical.

5. Third, there is a responsibility to ensure the required after-sales service, including dealing with a defective product. Certain practices to set the terms of warranty deliberately so as to make it practically impossible to enforce it are unethical, irrespective of their legal position.

6. In advertising, the ethical imperatives concern truthfulness in advertising, avoidance of obscene and offensive materials, non-denigration or maligning of competition, and being sensitive about the impact on society, especially young and impressionable minds, and relatively uneducated and uninformed target audiences.

7. Besides advertising, certain promotion practices (such as free samples to attract the audience to certain products) may also violate ethical norms.

REFERENCES

'Microsoft Litigation'. http://en.wikipedia.org/wiki/Microsoft_litigation, accessed on June 10, 2011.

'Subprime Lending'. http://en.wikipedia.org/works/subprime_lending, accessed on June 11, 2011.

Hoffman, M. 1984. 'The Ford Pinto', in Michael Hoffman and Jennifer Mills Moore (eds). *Business Ethics*. New York: McGraw Hill.

'India Debates "Racist" Skin Cream Ads'. http://news.bbc.co.uk/2/hi/south-asia/3089495.stm. July 24, 2003, accessed on June 11, 2011.

'Hindustan Unilever'. http://en.wikipedia.org/wiki/Hindustan_unilever, accessed on June 11, 2011.

'Infant Formula'. http://en.wikipedia.org/wiki/Infant_formula, accessed on June 12, 2011.

5

I Am the Boss: Employee Issues

> 'Regard your soldiers as your children, and they will follow you into the deepest valleys; look on them as your own beloved sons, and they will stand you even unto death.'
>
> —Sun Tzu, *The Art of War*

Employer–employee relations can be viewed on multiple planes. At one level they are contractual: the employer has engaged the employee for doing some jobs/rendering certain specified services to specified standards and in return the latter is compensated— partly through money, partly through perquisites, and partly through some intangibles. Here I use the term 'employer' to mean the representatives of the actual owner, supervising the work of an employee. This 'employer' himself may be an employee, of course, and acts as the agent of the owner, who, ultimately, is the employer. In theory, this is a non-coercive arrangement: the employer can terminate the employment, and the employee can quit, satisfying certain conditions. Thus, the relationship may appear to be symmetrical. But in reality, the relationship involves the exercise of highly asymmetrical powers by the employer over the employee for a variety of reasons, and this lies at the heart of ethical issues, besides the contractual/legal issues regarding employer–employee relationships. My focus is on these issues.

OBLIGATIONS OF AN EMPLOYEE

I first look at the issues regarding the obligations of an employee towards his organization. These are relatively less complex than the ones concerning employers.

First, of course, is the responsibility of an employee to discharge his duty as per the terms of employment, whether explicit or implicit: he ought to report for work at the appointed time, take breaks as allowed, depart only at the appointed time, and produce the required output. The other obligations include exercise of discipline, not engaging in activities that are disruptive, not damaging the equipment of the employer, and so on. He ought to carry out all lawful orders and point out to the company situations that may cause potential harm/damage to the organization. He is expected not to indulge in cheating regarding his output or other members of the organization.

Problems often arise due to real or perceived unfair exercise of power by the employer. In the absence of a proper grievance handling system or adequate communication by the employer, employees get frustrated, leading to alienation in the workplace. The employee discharges the legal requirements of his job, but has no 'connect' with the job or the organization. He develops apathy. His commitment to the work and the organization decreases; he 'stops caring'. The repetitive and dehumanizing nature of work in many situations (the assembly line is the best example of this alienation, see Box 5.1) exacerbates the problem.

BOX 5.1

The Unforgiving Assembly Line

The assembly line was basically the invention of Henry Ford to produce cars at such low prices as to make them affordable to every American. This was made possible through hugely enhanced productivity of the workers which, in turn, was made possible by their superspecialization in one job. Each worker would have one job to do through the day, such as tightening a bolt or doing spot welding. Over a day, this operation could get repeated some 10,000–20,000 times. The assembly moved on, unrelentingly, at its own pace. This led to major psychological and physical problems, as revealed in numerous studies, and the travails of the assembly line worker were immortalized in Charlie Chaplin's movie, *Modern Times* (1936).

The problems from the assembly line have been twofold: first, the highly repetitive, monotonous work, and second, the feeling of loss of control over the job: the helplessness when confronted with a relentlessly moving assembly line. Supervisors may want to help a worker with a problem but being a part of the system themselves, may be unable to. Everything is externally controlled, including visits to the toilet.

To mitigate such effects, job enrichment has been tried, with some success. The idea was an offshoot of the Hawthorne Experiments (see Box 5.2) which found that giving employees a certain control over the job as well as some job variety (so as to reduce monotony) actually increased productivity. Volvo conducted many experiments and today such enrichment is seen as having positive effects on employee productivity and morale.

BOX 5.2

The Hawthorne Experiments

The Hawthorne Experiments were carried out by Elton Mayo, Fritz Roethlisberger, and W.J. Dickson between 1924 and 1932 in one of the plants of Western Electric, USA, to investigate the effect of workplace lighting on employee productivity. A group of employees were selected for these experiments and they felt that they were specially selected people (although they were never told so). While the productivity increased with lighting, as expected, it continued to increase even after the lighting was restored to the old level, and then *reduced* even further. The researchers concluded that it was not so much the lighting that led to increased productivity as the feeling of the employees that they were special.

The experiments were continued in different versions. In some, the workers were given greater job variety (by giving them a module of work with different elements of operation), and the freedom to design their workplace and work content. This also enhanced their performance.

It is now accepted that 'de-alienation' of employees is beneficial to the employee and the organization.

From the employees' point of view, they need to accept that when they enter a workplace, there are some restrictions and inconveniences that go with it. This can lead to stress, anxiety, and even deterioration of health, but is it ethical to organize protests against the employers and coerce them into accepting new terms?

After knowingly having entered into a contract, it does not seem to be ethical to coerce the employer to alter it. But there

may be conditions where this behaviour could be accepted, as, for example, if the assembly line supervisor does not give breaks even to attend the call of nature, it would, sooner or later, lead to protest. The ultimate test here is fairness. If the employers' practices are unfair or unethical (as is the case with bonded labour) it may be necessary to protest in order to get rights.

Unionization, and subsequent phenomena such as strikes, violence, etc., may be the result of such unfair treatment over a long time, though unions themselves may be equally coercive towards their members. From an ethical perspective, organizing strikes and violence just to gain power would be as unethical as attempts to suppress such action through violence.

What Should You, as an Ethical Employee, Do?

You are bound to discharge your obligations as per the terms of employment and not cause intentional harm to property or to the good name of your employer. Due to the vast asymmetry in power, employers are prone to act unfairly, leading to alienation and protest actions. These may be justified under many circumstances but are to be considered as a last resort.

OBLIGATIONS REGARDING CONFLICTS OF INTEREST

Conflicts of interest arise when, as an employee, you are engaged in some activities on behalf of your organization, and the outcome of those activities would affect your private interests. An obvious example is if a purchase officer buys materials from a company he himself owns or one owned by his relatives. There is an *actual* conflict of interest if an employee purchases materials at inflated rates from a company owned by a relative so as to cause harm to the employer and benefit the relative's company. This is, of course, clearly unethical. *Potential* conflict of interest arises when you *could* influence the decision by being the decision maker, or if you are in a selection committee and one of the applicants is your close relative.

If such situations can be avoided, the ethical course is to avoid them, as, for example, by not sitting on those selection committees or purchase committees in which there is or could be a conflict of interest. The next best course would be to *disclose* the interest in the particular deal, besides being transparent about whatever decision is taken.

OBLIGATIONS REGARDING ILLEGAL GRATIFICATION

It is, of course, ethically reprehensible if you indulge in outright corruption. It is difficult to see when such behaviour could be ethically justified. Corruption is widely prevalent in India, not only in the government but also in the private sector. The problem comes when you try to define precisely what constitutes corruption.

No one would say that if a purchase officer visits a vendor's firm for any purpose and accepts a cup of tea it amounts to corruption. It is the same case with inexpensive gifts. Many companies lay down rules regarding acceptance of gifts by employees, sometimes specifying the maximum value of gifts acceptable. During certain times, as, for example, Diwali, quite expensive 'corporate gifts' are given to particular people of organizations, and whether accepting such gifts constitutes an unethical act would depend on the value of the gifts. But more than mere value, the critical test, from an ethical point of view, as to whether accepting such gifts is objectionable would be whether the gift is a precondition for effecting a particular deal. If the acceptor of the gift does not bestow or intend to bestow any undue favour on the giver, it may not be unethical (although the giver may expect favours in the future). Again, giving such gifts, especially on particular occasions such as Diwali may be customary in a society, and may be a part of the exchange of pleasantries in that society. Not carrying a gift to a first business meeting may be viewed very negatively in some societies, such as in Japan or Africa. There is absolutely no guarantee that by giving a gift a deal will be closed, but there is always the possibility that *not giving* such gifts may seriously jeopardize the deal and the long-term business relationship. But because such gifts do not explicitly form a condition for a favourable outcome, giving them may not fail in the ethical test. There is clearly a strong element of ethical relativism here, and hence it is difficult to lay down a categorical imperative on what should or should not be done.

It is, however, very unlikely that a business person spends money on lavish gifts if he is not likely to benefit from it. Hence, in the medium run, consistent receipt of such gifts by some persons in the organization would strongly indicate the possibility of their bestowing undue favours on some vendors (or others who deal with the firm).

What Should You, as an Ethical Employee, Do?

You need to employ the highest standards of integrity to avoid conflict of interest and not accept undue favours. The value of gifts received is important, but even more important is whether they are given as a precondition, explicit or implied, for the grant of some favours. The ultimate test for your behaviour is whether you are compromising the interests of your employer by your acts.

WHISTLEBLOWING

Whistleblowing is a particularly vexing issue because here the ethical course of action by an employee is far from clear.

Whistleblowing means the act of disclosing some information or acts of a company to people outside the company such as regulatory authorities, police, the public at large, etc. This clearly violates the principles of loyalty to the company and the need to keep certain matters confidential. But those who indulge in whistleblowing do so, in many (but not all) cases, due to their conviction that the company is causing serious harm to society and exposing them is a part of the employee's larger duty towards society. They may even believe that the organization is harming itself in the long run.

Here is where the conflict comes in. As an employee, you are expected not to do anything that causes harm to the organization. You may even have sworn to uphold confidentiality of information (as, for example, financial dealings). But the other issues are your larger duties towards society as a law-abiding citizen and perhaps the long-term interest of the organization itself (which might cleanse its top management and emerge stronger). There is also the issue to act in accordance with your conscience and not against it.

Examples of such situations could be numerous. A company may be cooking up its books to save on tax. It may be engaged in price fixing or unfair labour practices. It may be cooking up its books to deceive the shareholders, as was the case with Enron (see Box 5.3).

BOX 5.3

The Enron Saga

Enron, the company synonymous with corporate fraud on a gigantic scale, was founded in 1985 by Kenneth Lay. It grew spectacularly in the initial years, riding on the deregulation of electricity and gas prices. By 1992, it had become the largest seller of natural gas in North America. It also indulged in gas trading, and this business turned out to be profitable. But over a period of time it diversified into a number of businesses and adopted highly questionable accounting practices for revenue recognition, including the so-called mark-to-market accounting, where income was recognized based on the future cash flows of the contracts entered into, a maze of special-purpose vehicles, and so on. It 'managed' the Wall Street and its analysts very well, though few seemed to understand how exactly the firm made its profits. Those analysts who were sceptical of Enron's financial statements were attacked verbally and sought to be disgraced.

In August 2001 Sherron Watkins, Vice President Corporate Development sent an anonymous letter to Lay, warning him of the accounting problems in Enron. She contacted a friend who worked for Arthur Andersen, the firm's auditors, and informed him of her doubts. She did not tell any outsiders as such about the company, and hence it may not be accurate to call her a whistleblower in the true sense. But she did testify against Enron executives later, and her letter to Lay was produced as evidence in the trial of Enron's executives.

Sources: '"Person of the Week": Enron's Whistle Blower, Sherron Watkins', *Time*, January 18, 2002, http://en.wikipedia.org/wiki/Enron_scandal, accessed on April 28, 2011.

Was Watkins ethical in calling the attention of Lay, bypassing her seniors, and passing on her doubts to the people at Arthur Andersen? On the contrary, was she ethical in *not* making her letter public (in which case it would have surely saved numerous shareholders from ruin)?

Another famous whistleblowing case concerned Kermit Vandivier, who was employed in the testing wing of the B.F. Goodrich wheel and brakes plant in Troy, Ohio (see Box 5.4). The company had developed an innovative design for brakes for aircrafts for the air force, but these failed in tests. When fitted, these had not only the potential to cause serious accidents but also actually failed during actual field tests. Vandivier was coerced into falsifying the test data, and he eventually reported the entire episode publicly during subsequent Congressional investigation. He lost his job (while nothing serious happened to his bosses who had asked him to falsify the data).

BOX 5.4

The Aircraft Brakes Scandal

In 1967, Goodrich Company had received a contract to supply wheels and brakes for a new light combat aircraft for the US Air Force. Goodrich had bid for a new lightweight, four-rotor brake, replacing the then prevalent disc brakes. However, the company had to test the prototype and give the results to the Air Force. Unfortunately, all tests on the new brakes failed, and some in the company argued that it was a basic design problem that caused the failure. Another engineer, Lawson, who worked in the same department, and Vandivier repeatedly informed their superiors that the brakes were not withstanding the tests and something had to be done about the design, materials, and so on. Changing

---

than mere value, the critical test, from an ethical point of view, as to whether accepting such gifts is objectionable would be whether the gift is a precondition for effecting a particular deal. If the acceptor of the gift does not bestow or intend to bestow any undue favour on the giver, it may not be unethical (although the giver may expect favours in the future). Again, giving such gifts, especially on particular occasions such as Diwali may be customary in a society, and may be a part of the exchange of pleasantries in that society. Not carrying a gift to a first business meeting may be viewed very negatively in some societies, such as in Japan or Africa. There is absolutely no guarantee that by giving a gift a deal will be closed, but there is always the possibility that *not giving* such gifts may seriously jeopardize the deal and the long-term business relationship. But because such gifts do not explicitly form a condition for a favourable outcome, giving them may not fail in the ethical test. There is clearly a strong element of ethical relativism here, and hence it is difficult to lay down a categorical imperative on what should or should not be done.

It is, however, very unlikely that a business person spends money on lavish gifts if he is not likely to benefit from it. Hence, in the medium run, consistent receipt of such gifts by some persons in the organization would strongly indicate the possibility of their bestowing undue favours on some vendors (or others who deal with the firm).

What Should You, as an Ethical Employee, Do?

You need to employ the highest standards of integrity to avoid conflict of interest and not accept undue favours. The value of gifts received is important, but even more important is whether they are given as a precondition, explicit or implied, for the grant of some favours. The ultimate test for your behaviour is whether you are compromising the interests of your employer by your acts.

WHISTLEBLOWING

Whistleblowing is a particularly vexing issue because here the ethical course of action by an employee is far from clear.

Whistleblowing means the act of disclosing some information or acts of a company to people outside the company such as regulatory authorities, police, the public at large, etc. This clearly violates the principles of loyalty to the company and the need to keep certain matters confidential. But those who indulge in whistleblowing do so, in many (but not all) cases, due to their conviction that the company is causing serious harm to society and exposing them is a part of the employee's larger duty towards society. They may even believe that the organization is harming itself in the long run.

Here is where the conflict comes in. As an employee, you are expected not to do anything that causes harm to the organization. You may even have sworn to uphold confidentiality of information (as, for example, financial dealings). But the other issues are your larger duties towards society as a law-abiding citizen and perhaps the long-term interest of the organization itself (which might cleanse its top management and emerge stronger). There is also the issue to act in accordance with your conscience and not against it.

Examples of such situations could be numerous. A company may be cooking up its books to save on tax. It may be engaged in price fixing or unfair labour practices. It may be cooking up its books to deceive the shareholders, as was the case with Enron (see Box 5.3).

rates from a company owned by a relative so as to cause harm to the employer and benefit the relative's company. This is, of course, clearly unethical. *Potential* conflict of interest arises when you *could* influence the decision by being the decision maker, or if you are in a selection committee and one of the applicants is your close relative.

If such situations can be avoided, the ethical course is to avoid them, as, for example, by not sitting on those selection committees or purchase committees in which there is or could be a conflict of interest. The next best course would be to *disclose* the interest in the particular deal, besides being transparent about whatever decision is taken.

OBLIGATIONS REGARDING ILLEGAL GRATIFICATION

It is, of course, ethically reprehensible if you indulge in outright corruption. It is difficult to see when such behaviour could be ethically justified. Corruption is widely prevalent in India, not only in the government but also in the private sector. The problem comes when you try to define precisely what constitutes corruption.

No one would say that if a purchase officer visits a vendor's firm for any purpose and accepts a cup of tea it amounts to corruption. It is the same case with inexpensive gifts. Many companies lay down rules regarding acceptance of gifts by employees, sometimes specifying the maximum value of gifts acceptable. During certain times, as, for example, Diwali, quite expensive 'corporate gifts' are given to particular people of organizations, and whether accepting such gifts constitutes an unethical act would depend on the value of the gifts. But more may be conditions where this behaviour could be accepted, as, for example, if the assembly line supervisor does not give breaks even to attend the call of nature, it would, sooner or later, lead to protest. The ultimate test here is fairness. If the employers' practices are unfair or unethical (as is the case with bonded labour) it may be necessary to protest in order to get rights.

Unionization, and subsequent phenomena such as strikes, violence, etc., may be the result of such unfair treatment over a long time, though unions themselves may be equally coercive towards their members. From an ethical perspective, organizing strikes and violence just to gain power would be as unethical as attempts to suppress such action through violence.

What Should You, as an Ethical Employee, Do?

You are bound to discharge your obligations as per the terms of employment and not cause intentional harm to property or to the good name of your employer. Due to the vast asymmetry in power, employers are prone to act unfairly, leading to alienation and protest actions. These may be justified under many circumstances but are to be considered as a last resort.

OBLIGATIONS REGARDING CONFLICTS OF INTEREST

Conflicts of interest arise when, as an employee, you are engaged in some activities on behalf of your organization, and the outcome of those activities would affect your private interests. An obvious example is if a purchase officer buys materials from a company he himself owns or one owned by his relatives. There is an *actual* conflict of interest if an employee purchases materials at inflated the design was costly and time consuming. Vandivier and Lawson were asked to falsify the reports and distort the data. The doctored results were presented to the Air Force. The brakes were fitted on the aircraft for a field trial, and again they failed, putting the pilot's life in danger.

Vandivier informed the FBI agents of the discrepancies in the reports, and resigned from the company. He joined *Troy Daily News*, and eventually his revelations to the newspaper led to a Congressional investigation against Goodrich.

Sources: 'B.F. Goodrich Air Force A7-D Brake Problem Case and the Whistleblowing Debate', http://ethics.tamu.edu/ethics/goodrich/goodric1.htm, accessed on April 28, 2011; Kermit Vandivier, 'The Aircraft Brakes Scandal', in Thomas Donaldson and Patricia H. Werhane, (eds), *Ethical Issues in Business: A Philosophical Approach*, Englewood Cliffs, NJ: Prentice-Hall,1979.

Did Vandivier fail in his duty as an employee when he reported to the FBI and the daily as to what was going on? Should he have just gone along and risked jail if major failures took place and others let him down (as almost surely they would have)?

Whistleblowing may expose corruption in government and many powerful parties can be affected. Thus whistleblowing, whether ethical or not, could surely be dangerous. The law is also not clear, and efforts are being made to pass a law to protect whistleblowers. Undoubtedly, whistleblowing *could* be entirely self-serving and even be an attempt to cause harm to innocent persons.

What Should You, as an Ethical Employee, Do?

As an employee, you need to be clear about your motives while deciding to blow the whistle: first and foremost, the objectives should not be self-serving. Second, you need to be sure of the facts, and often these can be obtained from the company only through impermissible means (as the recent episodes of Wikileaks show), which itself constitutes an ethical misdemeanour. Hence only a compelling need can justify such a transgression. Third, you need to be clear as to what the ethical and societal issues involved in the case(s) are. Last, whistleblowing needs to be the final act, when it becomes clear that the company will not set right the wrongs on its own.

OBLIGATIONS OF AN EMPLOYER

In some ways, the obligations of an employer are a mirror image of those of an employee. In return for the efforts put in by the employee, the employer needs to compensate him in accordance with the contract, give the perquisites due to him and treat him fairly. But due to the unequal nature of the relationship, the employer has special obligations, some legal and some ethical.

Fair and Equitable Wages

Since often the applicant to a position is in need of the job to a much greater extent than the organization is in need of hands, the firm holds the upper hand in deciding the wages to be paid, as well as the terms and conditions of service. It is expected to pay a 'fair' wage. But what is a 'fair' wage? Perhaps what is the 'going rate' in the industry may be treated as a fair wage. Adjustments would need to be made for the nature of the job and the actual skill level of the applicant.

There can be no question that after having agreed to pay a wage, that wage should be given. Making an employee sign for a larger amount than is actually given, making unauthorized deductions, or unnecessary delays in payment are clearly unethical practices, although they are widely prevalent.

In organizations where there is organized labour, the wages for different categories of staff are usually fixed after negotiations with the unions or some representatives of the employees. The negotiations must be fair from both sides. This implies that unfair threat of lockout or other forms of blackmail are ethically not acceptable.

Promotions to employees are a feature of organizational life, and they should be based on a fair and transparent appraisal of an employee. 'Equitable' does not mean equal, but means bearing a relationship to the ability or contribution of a person. Thus appraisals need not give the same raises to everyone or promotions strictly by seniority, but rather appraise the actual performance of an employee against what is expected. The employee needs to be given an opportunity to have his say regarding the appraisal, and he should be informed of what the final appraisal was. Common unethical practices include arbitrary appraisals, appraisals based on parameters having nothing to do with the job, undue favouritism, failure to inform the appraisee, or even misinforming an employee (giving the impression that the assessment was good where in fact it wasn't), and not giving an opportunity to the employee to have his say.

Working Conditions: Health and Safety

Providing a safe working environment that does not affect the health of the employees is a prime requirement of an employer. This, at the base level, means appraising the physical risk involved in each job and providing the needed protective equipment. For example, welders need to be provided with suitable goggles that are certified, gloves and overalls; workers near steel-melting furnaces, foundries, and forge shops need to be given goggles, overalls and helmets, where there is a risk of falling objects, and so on. Should the company *enforce* the use of such equipment? Does it infringe on the freedom of the worker in allowing him to *not* use such equipment if he would prefer not to do so? This is a delicate question, but it would seem that, having overall responsibility for the safety of the workplace, organizations would not only be justified in enforcing the safety measures, but in fact have an obligation to enforce them. There is an implicit understanding that when an employee accepts a job, he should be subject to a certain discipline and should be willing to do the work in accordance with the procedures laid down, and the use of protective equipment is one of them.

There are certain occupational hazards of which the company is aware but which the workers may not be aware of. This is especially true in a country like India, where the majority of workers are not well educated and poor. They may not have the slightest notion of the hazards posed by the working conditions. Examples of these could be harm caused by asbestos inhalation and nuclear radiation. Since the effects are long term and it is not always easy to establish the linkage to the cause, the company could choose to look the other way and disown all responsibility for such events. In some cases, the employer may also be unaware, since the medical evidence linking to such hazards might emerge only later. The ethical position would be that the company needs to accept responsibility for the damage it has caused, and pay adequate compensation. But this is generally the exception than the rule, given the difficulty of establishing such linkages and the vastly superior ability of firms to fight legal cases as compared to that of their employees.

An ethical obligation of an organization is to conduct periodic medical check-ups for its employees, and if there are specific risks the employees are subjected to, conduct special tests to monitor their health for example, of those who work in radiation-prone jobs, and mines and traffic policemen manning traffic on roads (due to the pollution they are subjected to). It may also be a nice gesture on the part of organizations to provide suitable insurance cover, both general and job specific.

What Should You, as an Ethical Employer, Do?

As an employer, it is your obligation to pay fair wages as per employment agreements entered into and the norms, and be fair in assessment of employees for increments and promotions. It is also your ethical obligation to provide adequate safety and care for the health of your employees, and when risky jobs are involved, to give a risk premium for those jobs. You should proactively collect information regarding hazards due to chemicals, radiation, certain kinds of dust, etc. and ensure periodic health check-ups, besides giving insurance cover for your employees. Last, when incidence of health damage comes to light, you should compensate the employees adequately.

Employee Privacy Issues

Is an employee entitled to any privacy at all in the workplace? By privacy, I do not mean here an enclosed cabin or any such private place, but to his mail and other personal relationships. With the spread of e-mail, this has become a major issue: Is the company entitled to snoop into the e-mail sent by an employee from his workplace or the company server? Is the company entitled to open personal mail that might come to the official address? What about phone calls?

It may be argued that the employee is not supposed to do any private work in the office, including sending private e-mails. As a principle, of course, this cannot be disputed, but does it, by itself, give the company the right to intercept and read the mail?

In the pre-e-mail days, all the official mail sent or received by any employee was open and placed in files. Confidential letters were placed in special files and could be read only by those authorized to read them. But e-mail inboxes can contain personal data and mail and it is not clear if reading employees' e-mails does or does not impinge on his privacy. What if an employee is applying for another job from the present workplace? That is clearly unethical on the part of the employee, but *as a principle*, you still cannot approve of sneaking into the e-mail box of the employee. But it is becoming increasingly tough, and now with e-mail through smartphones, it has become even more difficult to track and catch e-mails by employees anyway.

It has now become a practical rather than an ethical issue. But this is not so with regard to enquiry into personal relationships between employees. Is the boss entitled to ask details about any affair an employee (or a couple) is having, on the ground that 'it is against company policy'? What about extramarital relationships? If a member of the top management is involved in a scandal, even though it does not relate to work or does not affect his efficiency in any way, is the company entitled to interfere and ask for details?

From an ethical perspective, enquiry into employees' personal affairs does constitute a violation of privacy, especially if these have no bearing on the organization's own work. Similarly, interfering in the employee's personal beliefs also is an invasion of privacy, especially if these beliefs are irrelevant as, for example, political beliefs, beliefs about God, religion, etc. But if they do, then these issues constitute a dilemma. Surely a priest cannot say he is a professionally competent priest but is an atheist. Nor can a buccaneering lifestyle be in tune with what is expected of a bank executive handling others' money.

These issues partly need to be addressed by laying down clear company policies. It may be difficult to enunciate clear-cut criteria for each one of such matters; much depends on the company, the organizational culture, and the people involved. Generally, it could be said that so long as the company's operations and reputation are not affected, it is best to leave the privacy of employees alone.

What Should You, as an Ethical Employer, Do?

You need to respect the privacy of the employees and seek to not violate it, unless it concerns or affects the operations of the organization. Regarding the personal affairs of your employees, again, it would be best to respect their right to privacy unless there are compelling reasons to not do so.

Discrimination among Employees

There is an obligation on the part of the employer to treat employees without discrimination, as a part of the overall responsibility for fair treatment. Discrimination takes place when there is adverse treatment meted out to an employee, not based on performance on job, but based on other parameters such as religion, ethnicity, region, social class, gender, etc. Though such discrimination is illegal, in most cases it is done extensively and subtly, and this makes it difficult to prove discrimination in most cases. Hence there is a need for the company to adopt, proactively, an ethical stance.

Two kinds of discrimination have become important recently: affirmative action through reservations based on caste, and gender discrimination.

Reservation is a touchy issue and I shall not enter into a philosophical debate about the ethics of a reservation policy itself. From the point of view of organizations, these are obligations laid down by law and, as such, they are required to follow these laws. The responsibility of organizations does not stop at the point of hiring; they need to help the weaker recruits acquire additional skills, otherwise they would face problems in getting promoted. There is always the question of some sacrifice in efficiency due to such reservations for if there is no such problem reservations would not be needed in the first place. In a competitive scenario, this is a tradeoff that companies would like to avoid. Yet the real costs of providing additional skills to weaker candidates could be quite less.

Gender discrimination and its concomitant evil, sexual harassment, have become important issues. It cannot be disputed that women are grossly underrepresented everywhere: in boardrooms, in the top management, and all the way down. There does seem to exist a glass ceiling which most women find hard to penetrate. But this by itself may not be evidence of discrimination. After all, a whole host of factors such as social attitude, lack of equal education opportunities at school and college levels, and taboos against women working in certain kinds of jobs could reduce the number of women applicants, to start with. Then women encounter barriers regarding the kinds of work they are assigned, working in night shifts, and so on. Marriage raises fresh problems, since continuation at work depends on the approval from a woman employee's husband and his family. Companies also have issues such as women having to miss work more often (for example, when children fall sick), and the need to give maternity leave.

Gender discrimination exists in wages in most countries where women are paid less than men for the same work. In the USA, surprisingly, the disparity in wages between men and women working at similar jobs seems to be more than in India. But even in India, discrimination exists, and escalates when women are due for promotion, for they are generally not seen as being equally competent as men (with a few exceptions). The problem is aggravated by men having attitudinal problems working under women.

These are the facts of life, and though ethically such discrimination is not acceptable, organizations tend to avoid too much of an unpleasant situation. Even the best organizations tend to balance the practical need for carrying on smoothly vis-à-vis the need not to discriminate.

A particularly vexing ethical issue is that of sexual harassment. Of course, an individual has an ethical duty not to indulge in such activities. Given the asymmetry of power, there is always the temptation to do so. As a manager, however, the ethical obligations are (a) to create a climate in which it is made clear that such activities will not be tolerated; and (b) to have a procedure for investigating complaints when they are made.

Creation of a healthy atmosphere at the workplace involves clear policies and statements of intent about intolerance of sexual harassment, and swift and exemplary action if cases of such harassment do occur. A periodic survey about how female employees feel about the atmosphere at the workplace, how safe they feel, and about the grievance redressal mechanisms would be of help in understanding the true situation on the ground.

Redressal mechanisms include having standing committees, the methods used for investigation by these committees, and procedures for appeal. Nowadays most large organizations have standing committees, usually chaired by a woman, and certainly with a fair share of women (it is assumed that women would have more empathy in such cases). The committee would need to be seen as functioning independently. Procedures for appeal would also need to be laid down.

The problem in dealing with such cases is that it is usually difficult to find evidence, due to obvious reasons. It comes to one person's word against another's, and cases are not uncommon where female employees frame their bosses who admonish them or give them negative appraisals. This can constitute sexual harassment and in reverse, harassing the boss with the threat of complaint. But, on the whole, it seems that since the power the boss has over his female subordinate tends to be high, this makes the latter vulnerable, and frequently when a female employee does complain, things would have reached quite a serious stage. It is here that the company needs to conduct a fair investigation.

What Should You, as an Ethical Employer, Do?

You need to install a proper mechanism to investigate into cases of discrimination, not just sexual harassment but all kinds of discrimination. But what is more important is to create a climate of non-discrimination. You need to adhere to the laws of the country and indeed try to give extra help to those who are weak. Gender discrimination needs to be dealt with more carefully, and sexual discrimination is something that cannot be tolerated.

Outsourcing

In order to enhance competitive advantage or simply to reduce costs, firms are increasingly resorting to outsourcing. The reduction in costs could result from the outsourced firm being more efficient or having lower costs due to its scale of operations (as, for example, the outsourcing of construction to construction companies or by Bharti Airtel outsourcing its operation, project execution, etc. to companies such as Siemens and IBM); usually cheaper costs result from the outsourced companies paying much less to their employees, with little or no benefits, bypassing laws regarding safety, compensation and other labour laws, and adopting questionable practices in their businesses. The outsourcing companies often shut their eyes to these issues, and take shelter under the contractual terms with the companies rendering service.

This position is increasingly being questioned by the courts as well as public opinion. The outsourcing firm is increasingly being held accountable for what is being done by the outsourced firm, including legal liabilities for accidents. Unfair exploitation by the outsourced firms is viewed as the liability of the outsourcer as well. For example, companies such as Nike have been targeted for outsourcing their work to countries such as Taiwan and China, where workers are alleged to be exploited. Similarly, firms outsourcing their IT work to countries such as India are scrutinized as to the labour and employee practices being adopted in those countries. Even procurement from such countries is scrutinized for their adherence to certain standards such as using child labour (see below), environmental degradation, and the kind of materials used in their inputs (even though they may satisfy the technical specifications). These may well be tactics used by Western countries to better their competitive position, but they need to be taken cognizance of.

Child Labour

This is another ethical issue that is gaining prominence. Child labour is banned in most countries, including India, but is widely practised. Firms employing labour adopt objectionable practices such as taking a family into bondage through loans and using their children, or simply purchasing their children who are effectively sold into lifelong slavery. They are kept under extremely oppressive conditions, including being locked up inside a factory for long hours, and being denied adequate food, rest etc. Some industries are notorious for using child labour, such as the garment, carpet weaving, fireworks, brassware and metalwork, and construction industries.

Sometimes it is made out that even though these industries are clearly exploiting children, the children and their families may indeed be worse off if they were not given any employment at all. Most of these families are extremely poor and have little education, and indeed the children may bring in income needed for the family to survive. Often these may be the only sources of employment in the area, and if the industries themselves close down, then it may worsen what may be a bad problem. Thus this argument has some validity, at least in the short run, but in the long run, this only leads to the perpetuation of the impoverished conditions of the poor families.

The other side of the problem is that while it is the general norm in those industries to adopt child labour and costs are kept down because of that, if one firm does not follow the practice, it may become uncompetitive and may even have to close down. Thus, the rules of the game are set not only by the companies themselves, but also by the competition. The ethical tradeoffs, though, are not clear.

What Should You, as an Ethical Employer, Do?

While you clearly need to observe the laws of the land with regard to employee treatment and child labour and go beyond to make sure the practices are legally correct, you also need to look at their basic fairness. Dealing with firms that employ questionable practices poses a special dilemma and each firm needs to define its policies in this regard. It is not possible to state a general rule regarding how to deal with such firms, since that depends on the nature of the actual practices adopted by these firms, the practices in the industry, and the standards you wish to set for yourself.

Ethical Issues in International Business

Certain peculiar issues could arise in international business when an employee resorts to or is left with no option other than indulging in unethical practices, or practices that may be considered unethical in the parent country. A typical problem is bribing for contracts. The Lockheed Scandal, discussed in Chapter 2, is an example of this kind of a dilemma. The companies, of course, emphasize their commitment to their ethical code as well as to the laws of the country, but in a competitive situation it does become a tricky business for an employee to choose between bribing and losing a contract. The local laws of a country also force companies to make drastic choices. Google faced a major problem in China (more on this in a later chapter), but one issue it faced was when a senior employee of Google, posted in China, gave iPods to Chinese officials, charging them to Google. In Chinese culture such gifts are considered routine and even expected, but this was a breach of US law (Foreign Corrupt Practices Act). The employee was fired by Google, though she was dumbfounded when she was called into the office of her senior and asked to leave. She just could not understand what wrong she had done (*Fortune*, May 2, 2011).

This is a typical case involving issues of ethical relativism, as discussed in Chapter 2. Bribing may not be seen as such at all in some societies, as was the case with the iPods. A company has to abide by the laws of the home country, and see how this can be managed in another country. Employees need to be briefed that whatever their personal beliefs regarding some practices may be, there are some core principles the company would not compromise on.

What Should You, as an Ethical Employer, Do?

Such situations are all too common in international business, and you need to make clear the company's policies and make sure that the employees understand them properly. These need to be consistent with the laws of both the country of incorporation and the country in which the company is operating.

CONCLUSION

There are legal obligations on the part of both employer and employee towards each other. Moreover, these are the ethical obligations. Satisfying legal requirements leads to compliance, but it is the way ethical obligations are framed and discharged that sets the climate and culture of an organization. It leads to better employee morale, which may lead to higher productivity. But, like all ethical questions, the ultimate justification is not whether the organization would gain, but it is that such behaviour is an end in itself. That is why it is not possible to set a uniform ethical code for all organizations; each organization needs to develop its own ethical code.

At the time of recruitment, organizations need to check whether the employees they are recruiting are in sync with their ethical code (whatever it is). If a new recruit does display a disconnect, the earlier he is discharged the better. For while lack of skills can be overcome through training and, to some extent, even certain attitudes, ethical orientation is generally difficult to change.

KEY TAKEAWAYS

1. When a person gets employed and becomes an employee, there are legal as well as ethical obligations on the part of both sides.

2. The employee has the obligation to do the work as required in the agreement, not to cause damage to the employer, and not act against the interests of the organization. Further obligations are not to be in situations where there is conflict of interest, and not to accept illegal gratifications.

3. Whistleblowing is a peculiar situation where the employee knowingly causes harm to the organization because he feels there is a larger purpose to be served. It is a tough call to take and depends on the circumstances.

4. The employer has the obligation to pay fair wages; not to cheat on these payments, exploiting the compulsions of the employee; and provide a safe working environment. Hazards need to be addressed and preventive and consequential obligations need to be recognized.

5. Privacy of the employees needs to be respected.

6. Discrimination is unethical, and it is the company's obligation to provide a suitable grievance redressal mechanism. Issues of sexual harassment are becoming increasingly important and need to be addressed.

7. Issues such as outsourcing and child labour pose special problems which firms need to be sensitive about.

8. International business raises peculiar issues and organizations need to lay down policies on what is acceptable and what is not.

REFERENCES

'"Person of the Week": Enron's Whistle Blower, Sherron Watkins'. 2002. *Time*, January 18. http://en.wikipedia.org/wiki/Enron_scandal, accessed on April 28, 2011.

Vandivier, K. 1979. 'The Aircraft Brakes Scandal', in Thomas Donaldson and Patricia H. Werhane (eds), *Ethical Issues in Business: A Philosophical Approach*. Englewood Cliffs, NJ: Prentice-Hall.

'B.F. Goodrich Air Force A7-D Brake Problem Case and the Whistleblowing Debate'. http://ethics.tamu.edu/ethics/goodrich/goodric1.htm, accessed on April 28, 2011.

'Google and Its Ordeals in China'. 2011. *Fortune*. May 2.

6

Dealing with 'Them': Ethics towards Competitors

'The only sustainable competitive advantage is the ability to learn faster than the competition.'
—Arie de Geus, author of *The Living Company* (1997)

Compared to all the constituencies I have dealt with so far, dealing with competitors may perhaps seem the hardest. Can you deal ethically with competition at all, especially in today's hyper-competitive world? What do you do when the competition is not ethical (and most of the time, a company would come across competitors who are not ethical)? When everyone is cheating, can a company play by the rules? If it loses to competitors, who will answer the shareholders?

These are legitimate and very important questions. A company can decide to be ethical but it cannot compel its competitors to also be ethical. Then the playing field gets uneven, the arena gets distorted, and all are playing the foul game.

There is no question that the first priority of a firm is to survive, to be 'ongoing'. Is there such a thing as ethically losing a battle? The dilemma was brought out in the *Mahabharata* in which Krishna disposes of the major Kaurava opponents in the war through means that may be called unethical. Thus Bhishma is eliminated by putting Shikhandi in the chariot in front of Arjuna; Drona is told a falsehood, definitely with the intention to deceive, about his son's death and is killed when he is in a state of shock; Karna is killed when his chariot sinks into soft ground and he tries to get it out; and Duryodhana is killed by Bhima by hitting his thighs (not permitted). When lying immobilized and living his last moments, Duryodhana asks Krishna about the dharmic pretensions of the latter, considering that the war was won by basically using many adharmic means. Krishna simply tells him that he had to win the war; it would not do much good if, at the end, the war was lost.

But that does not mean *anything* goes, there are no rules to play by. I shall look at some situations where ethical issues arise while dealing with competitors. The main areas include:

(a) pricing;

(b) advertising;

(c) intelligence gathering;

(d) playing dirty tricks and damaging competitors' reputation; and

(e) poaching employees from the competition.

PRICING

The first issue in pricing is pricing a product unfairly *low* with a view to driving out the competition. This is usually resorted to by firms that have dominant market power or strong financial muscle. The idea is not to increase the value to the customer, for, in such a case, the practice can be justified. Since a cheaper product is offered to the consumers the overall welfare is increased, and it may also stimulate efforts to increase efficiency by the competition. The problem comes when the idea is to first drive out the competition, increase market share, and then use the increased market power to push up the prices to levels higher than they were before. Firms at times even sell below cost with a view to recover the losses later. This kind of pricing is called predatory pricing, indicating the intention to be a predator on the competitors.

Governments can investigate such instances but these are usually difficult to prove, especially if the firm has a multitude of products and other products are used to cross-subsidize the particular product predatorily priced. In most cases, costs are difficult to establish by an outside agency. This explains why this practice is so common.

From an ethical point of view, however, such practices are not defensible. They infringe on the right of another firm to enter and conduct business fairly. Faced with such an onslaught, the new entrants may indeed bring new technologies, practices, and customer value in some cases but, more often, such practices infringe on the customers' right to have a better choice, and may perpetuate inefficiency. Thus, from a consequentialist point of view again, it fails the test. Sometimes such pricing may lead to retaliation by others, leading to the industry itself going sick. Hence the general consequence of such actions is overall loss of welfare, and the need for many new entrants and small firms to exit.

Firms resorting to such tactics are willing to face short-run losses to gain a much bigger advantage in the medium and long run. But the firms may lose even in the medium run since governments and competition regulatory authorities have become sensitive to such practices. Firms may also quietly start compromising on quality due to pressure on profits, leading to a loss of reputation in the long run.

When resorted to in international trade, the practice of selling below cost is called 'dumping'. Many countries investigate charges of dumping and impose countervailing duties to counter the artificially lower prices. Countries such as Japan, Korea, and, recently, China have been accused of dumping and, in several cases, countervailing duties have been imposed. Japan was accused for a long time of dumping its steel; now China is accused of dumping not only steel but a whole variety of manufactured products. Under the rules of the World Trade Organization, such dumping is prohibited but usually it is very difficult to prove dumping due to the difficulty in getting reliable cost data.

Then there is the issue of pricing high to take advantage of a monopoly situation. In a dominant market share situation, there are usually regulators to see that firms do not misuse monopoly power. But it is common that when one of the players in an industry has a strike, the competitors take advantage by hiking fares to clearly unreasonable levels as happened, for example, when the pilots of Air India went on strike (Indian airline companies seem to have a particularly high tendency to cash in on a situation created by a strike in one of the competing airlines). Pharmaceutical companies have a virtual monopoly over certain drugs because they have some products that are much more efficient than those of the competitors (as, for example, certain drugs for cancer, tuberculosis, and AIDS treatment), and thus constitute an effective monopoly. Often pharmaceutical companies are seen to be pricing the drugs as far too high, although they claim that they need to recover their R&D and testing costs. A peculiar problem in the pharmaceutical industry is that many drugs are lifesaving, and it is seen as unethical in depriving patients of treatment and letting them die if they cannot afford the medicine.

Last, there is the practice of price fixing. Though this violates competition laws in most countries, the practice is seen to be widespread, especially when the industry is concentrated with few competitors. Here it is really not a question of ethics towards competitors, but being unethical in joining hands with them. A moot question: Is it unethical to enter into a cartel and then quietly indulge in underpricing? Perhaps not, because the decision to enter into the cartel itself is unethical.

ADVERTISING

I showed in Chapter 4 the ethical issues involved in advertising in general. Here I look only at those issues that are relevant vis-à-vis the competition.

The most obvious issue is regarding whether a firm needs to talk about competing products at all. This was generally looked down upon in the advertising industry; an obvious risk is that of legal suits by the competition. What is definitely not ethical is the denigration of competitors' products, giving a deliberately unfair picture. Usually products can be compared on multiple dimensions; consciously choosing one dimension and using it to compare the products may not be ethical, even if the comparison is factually correct. For while the claim may be true with respect to one dimension (say, size), it overlooks other dimensions (such as reliability) that may be better in the competitor's products. Misleading propaganda against a competitor's product is clearly unethical. Sometimes such propaganda is not explicit but is still done with the clear intention of evoking a misleading, poor image of a competing product. The most common examples are advertisements for washing detergents, comparing the company's product against that of 'a competitor', and though the competing brand is usually not mentioned, the packaging is made to clearly resemble that of the competing brand. Soft drinks manufacturers also often resort to such advertising.

Sometimes the advertisement is in good humour and good taste as, for example, the famous series of advertisements by Pepsi during the Wills World Cup, 1997. Pepsi had bid for the official sponsorship of the game and lost to Coca-Cola, which promptly splashed out all over the media about being the official supplier of soft drinks for the game. Pepsi cashed in on the rebelliousness of youth and roped in the then upcoming cricketer Sachin Tendulkar with the line 'There is nothing official about it'. No explicit reference was made to Coca-Cola, but the implicit reference was obvious, and yet no one could describe it as distasteful or unethical.

Often when advertisements claim 'they are the best' or they are the 'sole' products to have some attribute, they make themselves liable not only to legal challenges but charges of being unethical. Much depends upon what is said and how it is said. A good example is the controversies over the advertisements by the sugar substitute Sugar Free and Nutralite, both involving Zydus Cadilla and Gujarat Cooperative Milk Marketing Federation (GCMMF), the owners of the brand name Amul (see Box 6.1).

BOX 6.1

Sugar Free and Nutralite

Zydus Cadila of Ahmedabad has a sugar substitute which is based on aspartame, and has much fewer calories than sugar. The name of this product is Sugar Free. It is marketed in packets and capsule boxes, to be used as a sweetener. GCMMF, which owns the well-known brand Amul, launched a sugar-free ice cream, which it advertised as 'sugar free'. Zydus objected to this and filed a suit seeking to restrain Amul from using the phrase; Amul was

---

restrained from using it as a term which might connect the customers to Zydus' brand (Amul did not use the product Sugar Free in its ice cream). Subsequently, however, the court held that the mere term 'sugar free' could not be viewed as a trademark and hence Amul could use this term in its advertisements for its ice cream, but not use it as a trademark.

The second controversy was regarding a vegetable oil-based butter named Nutralite, introduced by Zydus Cadila. This contained little cholesterol and was therefore projected as a healthy substitute for traditional butter. Zydus ran a series of humorous advertisements showing a person looking forward to his favourite menu—aloo paratha and pav bhaji—that needs butter but, being health conscious, he has to (reluctantly) forgo them. His wife comes up with excuses as to why she cannot also prepare the dishes that day. Finally, one day, he is offered his favourite items (using Nutralite) and the advertisement ends showing him having a hearty meal with no anxiety.

The problem with this advertisement was that it claimed that Nutralite was 'better than butter'. Amul took objection to this, and later Zydus changed its advertisement to 'healthier than butter'.

Both these advertisements probably did not involve any real intention to deceive, but they show how thin the line you walk on could be when advertising your products vis-à-vis those of competitors.

Sources: 'Amul Loses its Sugar-free Market', http://www. downtoearth.org.in/node/5875, accessed on June 22, 2011; 'A Brand Analysis on Nutralite (Better than Butter)', http://www. scribd.com/doc/19149965/Nutralite-is-better-than-butter-Marketing-Case, accessed on June 22, 2011.

INTELLIGENCE GATHERING

All companies need intelligence about what the competitors' plans are so that they can take proactive action. This is done through a variety of ways, such as gleaning hints of intention through published annual reports, statements by the top management, press releases, and information gained in informal conversations at parties.

This, of course, is usual business practice. The ethical angle comes in when firms resort to other covert activities to glean information about competitors. One way is to have some contacts (or moles) in the other companies whose function it is to pass on information and probably get paid. Another way is to poach an employee (see the next section as well), with or without the intention of getting inside information. Firms try to prevent employees from carrying out such acts through various means including prohibition of taking up employment with a competitor for a period and even initiating legal action against the employee and the competing firms if they violate the agreement. Whatever be the legal outcome it seems clear that, from an ethical point of view, such practices cannot be approved.

PLAYING DIRTY TRICKS AND DAMAGING COMPETITORS' REPUTATION

This is a common activity but there can be no debate about the ethical nuances of such actions. These involve activities such as spreading baseless rumours about a competitor or making unfounded observations on a firm's functioning, influencing regulators to specifically hurt a firm, getting investigations launched against the competitors, and so on. The best example of the deadly effect of such activities would be banking. It is well known that if a bank is rumoured to have solvency problems, there will be a run on the bank and it will indeed become insolvent. The attack on ICICI Bank three years back led to its ATMs being raided in an unprecedented fashion, and it was only due to the determined action on the part of the top management (and support from the government) to restore confidence that a serious problem was averted. When Virgin Atlantic started its operations across the Atlantic, the big-brother incumbent, British Airways, spread rumours about the safety of its aircraft, training of its pilots and crew, its alleged (but untrue) non-refund policies, and so on. Richard Branson, CEO, Virgin Atlantic, sued British Airways and won a settlement. A soft drinks business owner in India was alleged to have bought up the competitors' drinks in large quantities and broken the bottles to deprive the latter of bottles and hence of sales. You can find a number of such instances simply by reading the newspapers.

POACHING OF EMPLOYEES

Poaching generally refers to inducing an employee of a competing company to leave the company and join the firm, generally through a promise of much higher remuneration. Movement from one company to another is normal, as long as it is within limits. But when resource talent is scarce in an industry, this becomes a game that hurts everyone. Often, firms in an industry agree upon a 'non-poaching' policy but, like cartels, such agreements do not last long.

It is, in fact, very difficult to prevent employee migration, and it is also perfectly legitimate for a firm to negotiate (obviously, such negotiations need to be discreet and even secretive) with employees of other firms, and such migrations take place away from a firm as well as into it. It becomes a problem if it leads to serious difficulties in the industry, with employees constantly switching from one company to another, as happened in the Indian IT industry. However, it is difficult to specify the yardstick or a rigid rule for the ethical limit in such cases.

What Should You, as an Ethical Manager, Do?

You need to recognize that there *are* ethical and non-ethical ways of competing, some of which may be legal but still do not pass the test of ethics. Some unethical ways have been described above. It is definitely not the case that competitors are there to be demolished, and that any action is justifiable while fighting the competition.

As an ethical manager, you could take care in pricing, neither engaging in predatory pricing to drive out competition nor abusing your monopoly power to fix the price at extortionate levels. In advertisements, while it is perfectly fine to extol the virtues of your product (provided it is true, of course), you should not consciously denigrate the competitor's product, however clever this denigration is.

You should do your own intelligence gathering, but using unfair means to spy on competitors should surely be avoided. Poaching is usually acceptable as long as it is within limits. Finally, dirty tricks need to be avoided; from a practical point of view, they invite dirtier tricks.

WHAT IF YOUR COMPETITORS ARE UNETHICAL?

I am sure many of you are saying, 'All this is fine, but this is the real world, and we have to play the game accordingly. I can be ethical towards my competitors, but that does not mean my competitors will be ethical. For example, I can avoid poaching employees, but what do I do if the competitor is poaching from me?'

These are legitimate questions. It is true that business is not always a clean game (nothing in life is!), and there are many sharp practices and crooked players. After all, if you are a boxer, you cannot avoid punching.

One way of understanding what to do in such situations is to use the insights of Game Theory, originally formulated by John von Neumann and Oskar Morgenstern and contributed to in a substantial measure by John Nash (the same Nash as was portrayed in the film *A Beautiful Mind* [2001]). Game Theory assumes the competition acting in a particular way, depending on its self-interest and *how you act in response*. The best way to understand it is through the game of Prisoners' Dilemma (see Box 6.2).

BOX 6.2

Prisoners' Dilemma

Imagine two prisoners have been arrested and put in two separate cells. They cannot see each other or communicate. The police have no real evidence against either of them, but induce them to confess through a deal. If one of them ('A') confesses, he can go free, and the other ('B') will get a jail sentence of ten years. Ditto if B confesses. If both confess, they will get a lighter sentence of seven years each. If neither confesses, they will be kept in jail for one year (pending investigations) and then released. The choices and outcomes are seen in Figure 6.1.

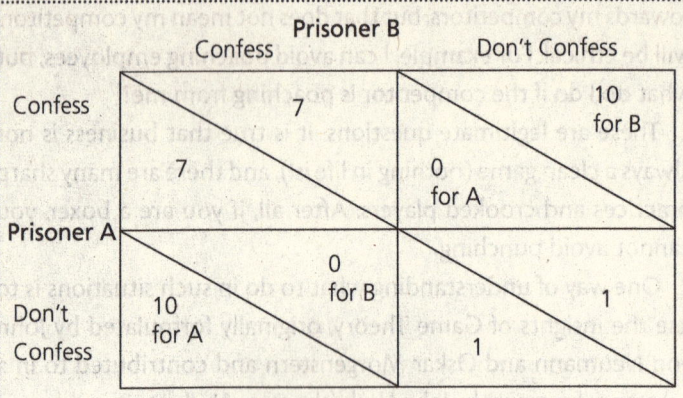

Figure 6.1

Prisoners' Dilemma: Payoff Matrix

In each cell, the southwest half represents the payoff for A and the northeast half for B.

What is the best strategy for the prisoners? Clearly, from their point of view, if both do not confess, that will be the best outcome for both. But can they rely on each other? If A trusts B and does not confess and then B ditches him, A will be worse off. Thus the safe thing for A is to confess, and the same for B. A is better off confessing (as compared to not confessing), *no matter what B does*. The same holds good for B versus A.

The game is usually never played just once but repeated over rounds. In classrooms, the jail terms may be replaced with positive or negative rewards. Now at each round, the dilemma remains the same and is *not dependent* on what has happened in the previous rounds, and it may seem that both A and B will go on confessing. This is assuming a strictly rational model of decision making. In fact, this rarely happens. Since A and B know that there is a next round and there could be retaliation (or mutually beneficial collaboration), they assess each other's reliability and once confidence is gained, both do not confess (of course once in a while there is a temptation to cheat), and this usually invites retaliation in subsequent rounds, trust being restored only after quite a while. Once you have demonstrated your weak ethics, the climb back to a higher moral ground is hard.

Interestingly, in most of the games (played in different cultures and types of audiences), the dominant strategy both players arrive at tends to be one of mutual cooperation (implied and developed, since they cannot communicate or negotiate), with the understanding that *if one side cheats, there will be retaliation*. This is indeed how alliances and joint ventures work and provide a basis for ethical dealings.

Much, however, depends on the structure of the payoff matrix. Suppose the matrix is modified as shown in Figure 6.2. As earlier, the southwest diagonal half of each square represents the consequences for A and the northwest diagonal half for B. What is the strategy for A and B? I leave that as an exercise for you.

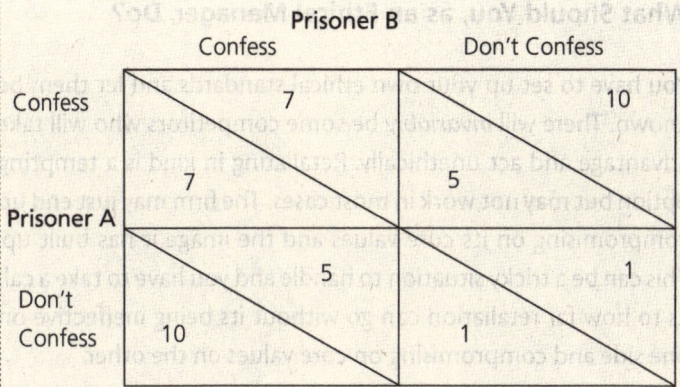

Figure 6.2: 'The Criminal's Revenge'

Source: John Kay, *Foundations for Corporate Success*, Oxford: Oxford University Press, 1993, pp. 35–9.

Thus while dealing with competitors, going solely by your own standards may not work, if the competitor indulges in unfair and unethical practices and knows he can get away with it. It would be better to follow the rule, 'I would go by my ethical standards so long as you, the competitor, do not take advantage of me to hurt me. But if you do, there will be retaliation.'

A question can be raised: Can you change your ethical standards if others are unethical? Would being unethical yourself be a suitable response to an unethical competitor?

The answer is that retaliation does not necessarily mean unethical retaliation. There may be legal and ethical ways of doing so. Initiating legal proceedings may be one device; for example, a deliberately misleading advertisement can be stopped from being aired through a court injunction. The affected firm could issue clarificatory statements. If a firm retaliates unethically, its moral foundation is undermined and its credibility lost.

What Should You, as an Ethical Manager, Do?

You have to set up your own ethical standards and let them be known. There will *invariably* be some competitors who will take advantage and act unethically. Retaliating in kind is a tempting option but may not work in most cases. The firm may just end up compromising on its core values and the image it has built up. This can be a tricky situation to handle and you have to take a call as to how far retaliation can go without its being ineffective on one side and compromising on core values on the other.

CONCLUSION

Ethics towards competitors is especially difficult to handle as a subject because, unlike others, in the case of competitors, it is not possible to lay down the rules, and what you should do depends on what others do (though Kant may not agree with this). So ethics need to be a standard for yourself but there also need to be in place deterrents to competitors from acting unethically in such a manner that it seriously hurts your firm.

I have discussed some situations and possible responses as, for example, in pricing, advertising, intelligence gathering, playing dirty tricks, and poaching of employees from other firms. Each of them (except playing dirty tricks) involves ethical dilemmas and issues and, as in the case of other stakeholders I have dealt with earlier, the firm and its top management need to take a stand and decide on how they should meet these situations.

Dealing with competitors is especially tricky because of two reasons. First, there are no ways to enforce ethical behaviour. Second, what you need to do depends on what the competitors do. Hence it is indeed very difficult to say how you should act ethically, since it depends so much on the nature and magnitude of the competitors' moves. Yet you need to establish a balance between making an effective response that at least deters the competitors from making unethical moves.

KEY TAKEAWAYS

Dealing with competitors is especially difficult from an ethical point of view and poses unique issues.

1. The issues arise at least in five areas: predatory pricing, unethical advertising aiming at tarnishing the reputation of competitors, gathering intelligence about competitors through unfair means, playing what may be called dirty tricks, and poaching employees from other firms, especially your competitors.

2. In each of the situations, each firm needs to set its own standard of behaviour and make it known to employees, competitors, and the outside world.

4. Dealing with unethical competition is indeed a major problem. Usually the solution is not equally unethical. However, effective responses that do not involve any compromises on ethics can often be found.

REFERENCES

'Amul Loses Its Sugar-free Market'. http://www.downtoearth.org.in/node/5875, accessed on June 22, 2011.

'A Brand Analysis on Nutralite (Better than Butter)'. http://www.scribd.com/doc/19149965/Nutralite-is-better-than-butter-Marketing-Case, accessed on June 22, 2011.

De Geus, A. 1997. *The Living Company*. Boston, MA: Harvard Business School Press.

Kay, J. 1993. *Foundations for Corporate Success*. Oxford: Oxford University Press.

7

The Firm and its Environment

'What is the use of a fine house if you haven't a tolerable planet
to put it on?'

—Henry Thoreau

In this chapter, I look at the issues regarding a firm and its physical environment such as air, water, forest and green space, etc. Pollution is a necessary by-product of industrialization. In fact, the environment is affected even by human existence and that of flora and fauna—by breathing, excretion, and consumption of resources. But nature seems to have a wonderful capability for self-correction—thus carbon dioxide breathed out by humans and animals is breathed in by plants for photosynthesis. This self-regenerating capacity continued for a long time in our history, but industrialization brought in an altogether new dimension in our relationship with the environment. First, the requirements of raw materials such as coal, metal ores, oil, wood and so on increased vastly. The second has been the sheer increase in the scale of consumption of existing materials such as water. The third has been the emission of smoke and industrial by-products on a new, huge scale. Last, it has led to the production of completely new toxic substances hitherto unknown.

Of course, the benefits of industrialization are there for all to see. What can be loosely described as 'quality of life' would have been impossible but for this industrialization. In a sense, this is the price mankind has to pay for the increased comforts it is now possible to enjoy. But, from the ethical point of view, in general, the beneficiaries of such activities tend to be different from those who have to pay the price: the former tend to be rich people, while the suffering is for the poor. Thus, though from a utilitarian perspective it may be justified to have pollution if its consequences are outweighed by the benefits to the society as a whole, it clearly goes against the test of justice. Some argue that even from the utilitarian perspective this is not justified because *in the long run*, the costs may outweigh the benefits. Then there is the issue of sustainability, and of responsibility to the future generations. But it is not clear if the present generation needs to suffer beyond a point to benefit the future unborn generations.

Having said this, it is still clear that reduction of damage to the environment is highly desirable. To force firms to adhere to some standards, countries have enacted laws regarding pollution standards, standards to ensure continuing protection to natural ecological structures, and standards by which certain resources such as water can be used. That is as far as the legal requirements go. From an ethical point of view, however, I argue that a firm needs to look at not only mere compliance to such laws as may be prevalent, but go *beyond* and ensure that it does its best to keep its pollution as low as possible and that it does not affect the rights of others in society. I shall look at these aspects in greater detail in this chapter.

ISSUES IN POLLUTION

The central problem with pollution is what economists call the *externalities* the actions taken at the firm level entail. When a firm emits smoke, for example, the pollution so caused may affect the community in its vicinity in many forms: for example, carbon soot gets deposited in homes, and health problems such as breathing difficulties are created. But the community members so affected reap the consequences and incur the costs, not the firm. These are called negative externalities: while the benefits are appropriated by the firm, some or all of the costs are not incurred by the firm. (Positive externalities also may exist. For example, when a factory is set up in a backward area, many supporting activities may also come into existence, such as schools and hospitals, and due to a general increase in commercial activity, the general income levels of the community may go up). Similar is the case with water pollution: if a firm discharges harmful chemicals into a river, the drinking water supply of the community gets affected, and serious ailments can ensue. The firm bears no consequences for its actions and has no incentives to reduce the pollution it causes.

The problem is tackled at the policy level by framing different laws to curb pollution. The standards for pollution are prescribed and firms monitored for compliance. But what should these standards be? What kinds of pollution are considered acceptable, and how much? Who decides? All said and done these are ultimately arbitrary decisions and could vary from country to country, and even in one country, from region to region and from time to time. There are also the inevitable costs associated with pollution control: the equipment and processes needed to control pollution entail costs and, at times, considerable costs. It may be argued that the costs a developed country can afford cannot be afforded by a developing country. There could also be legacy costs. One company or companies in one country might have old equipment that is highly polluting but these cannot be replaced overnight by better and less polluting equipment. Government policies need to take all these factors into account.

Pollution might be caused by a firm both directly, that is, through emissions from its own factories, and indirectly through its products. For example, a cement company or a coal burning power plant tends to be quite polluting from their own plants. A coal mining company may not itself be polluting but its product, namely, coal, is a big pollutant. Cars and two-wheelers produced by automobile manufacturers contribute to pollution indirectly due to emissions. In the former case, pollution standards need to be prescribed for the firms themselves; in the latter case, standards need to be set for their products as, for example, pollution norms for cars.

Air Pollution

Air pollution comes through multiple sources. The first is smoke which gives rise to unburnt carbon as soot, and gases such as carbon dioxide and carbon monoxide. Of these, carbon dioxide is naturally absorbed by plants and converted into oxygen, thus replacing the oxygen lost through burning of fuels. But there are two factors influencing this delicate equilibrium. First, with increased industrialization, the emissions themselves increase, and it has been argued that big industrializing countries such as China and India have a special 'responsibility' to reduce future emissions. But this argument is countered by the argument that the per capita emission in these countries is far less than that in developed countries: for example, the per capita consumption of resources by India is hardly one-thirtieth of that by the USA. Different rounds of discussions are going on in world forums to tackle the issues and arrive at a consensus as to who is to do how much.

The problem is becoming urgent due to *climate change*. Many scientists feel that the carbon dioxide emitted by industrial activity, in addition to the normal biological activities of living beings, rises up in the atmosphere and forms a greenhouse, the so-called *greenhouse effect*. This greenhouse traps the heat in the earth, preventing it from escaping into space, causing *global warming*. Scientists link many natural changes such as temperature, rainfall, etc. to the effects of this climate change.

Another major issue is that of chlorofluorocarbons (CFCs). These were used extensively in aerosol sprays and refrigerators. CFCs are non-degradable and rise up into the atmosphere, and break down the ozone molecules which form a protective cover to the earth, blocking the sun's ultraviolet rays. Breakdown of the ozone layer has been documented, especially over Antarctica, and CFCs are considered as contributing to the melting of Antarctica's glaciers. Today, CFCs have been phased out after the Montreal Protocol, and are not used for the above applications. But there may still be many similar compounds that may contribute to the ozone layer depletion and greenhouse gases.

The problem of global warming and allied environmental problems were highlighted in the famous Academy Award-winning documentary, *An Inconvenient Truth* (2006). Directed by Davis Guggenheim, the film is the outcome of the passionate efforts made by former US Vice President Al Gore, and brings out vividly the problems of climate change and pollution (see Box 7.1).

BOX 7.1

An Inconvenient Truth

The documentary film *An Inconvenient Truth* was the outcome of the crusading zeal of Al Gore, as revealed in a presentation that he made a large number of times to raise public awareness about the issues of global warming and climate change. It was produced in 2006 and received rave reviews (and record earnings for a documentary). Al Gore has also written a book with the same name.

The former vice president opens the film by greeting an audience with a joke: 'I am Al Gore; I used to be the next President of the United States.' He continues the show with numerous charts, statistics, and flowcharts to show how climate change is here with us, and how it will affect us all. There are majestic photographs of the earth, showing it as a planet too good to be laid waste.

Throughout the movie, Gore discusses the scientific opinion (or, rather, the different opinions) on climate change, as well as the present and future effects of global warming. He stresses that climate change 'is really not a political issue, so much as a moral one'. He effectively puts forth the consequences he believes global climate change will produce if the amount of human-generated greenhouse gases is not significantly reduced in the very near future. Gore also presents Antarctic ice-coring data showing carbon dioxide levels higher now than in the past 650,000 years.

The film includes segments intended to refute critics who say that global warming is unproven or that it will be insignificant. For example, Gore discusses the possibility of the collapse of a major ice sheet in Greenland or in West Antarctica, either of which could raise global sea levels by approximately 20 feet (6 metres), flooding coastal areas and producing 100 million refugees. Recently, one of the large glaciers of West Antarctica were found to have broken off, and this was not so much due to the warming from *above*, but from *below*, that is, from the seas. Water that has melted from Greenland because of its lower salinity could halt the currents that keep northern Europe warm and quickly trigger dramatic local cooling there. It also contains various short animated projections of what could happen to different animals more vulnerable to climate change.

The documentary ends with Gore arguing that if appropriate actions are taken soon, the effects of global warming can be successfully reversed by releasing less carbon dioxide and planting more vegetation to consume the existing carbon dioxide. Gore calls upon his viewers to learn how they can help him in these efforts. He concludes the film by saying:

> Each one of us is a cause of global warming, but each one of us can make choices to change that with the things we buy, the electricity we use, the cars we drive; we can make choices to bring our individual carbon emissions to zero. The solutions are in our hands, we just have to have the determination to make it happen. We have everything that we need to reduce carbon emissions, everything but political will. But in America, the will to act is a renewable resource.

Sources: Al Gore (dir.), *An Inconvenient Truth* (2006); 'An InconvenientTruth',http://en.wikipedia.org/wiki/An_Inconvenient_Truth, accessed on June 24, 2011.

I have highlighted these issues concerning pollution so that you get a perspective of the problem, and the actions needed at the firms' level (rather than at the policy level) can be highlighted. Since so much is really determined at the policy level, it is difficult to see what an individual firm can do and contribute, but as I shall argue later, there are many actions that go beyond merely conforming to legal requirements and reach out into the ethical plane. Before I come to a discussion of these actions, a review of the other kinds of pollution would be useful, since I will consolidate my arguments for action for different kinds of pollution later.

Water Pollution

Pollution of water has increased dramatically in recent years with the emergence of different industries, especially the chemical industry and industries that use chemicals (such as the paper industry). Many chemical processes, such as the purification of ores, require large quantities of water, and release a variety of toxic chemicals. Most of these chemicals were routinely discharged into rivers, since this was most convenient. Often discharges were also made into the sea, as mentioned in the case of Zuari Agrochemicals in Chapter 2. These affect the health of not only the users of this water, but also that of other water creatures, mostly fish. Today, treatment processes are available; these can treat the effluents and also enable firms to reuse the water, at a cost, of course.

Sometimes even unpolluted water discharged at high temperatures, can lead to the destruction of fish and other water creatures. Certain kinds of pollution are known to have long-term effects and there are others whose effects are not precisely known.

Another recent problem is the pollution of groundwater as well as its depletion (as discussed in the case of Coca-Cola in Plachimada in Chapter 1). Often, in an effort to show zero pollution in rivers, firms resort to pumping back the polluted effluents into underground water which, unlike flowing rivers, spread slowly and far and wide. The problem is especially serious since it is often not possible to prove who is responsible for this pump back.

Oil spills have become a major source of pollution in seas. The recent series of oil spills, such as the one in the Gulf of Mexico by British Petroleum and the Alaska oil spill, have drawn attention to the huge scale of damages involved, and costs such as for the clean-up and giving compensation to those affected. Despite claims by the oil exploration industry, the risk of such spills seems to be high and with the increasing depths from which oil is drilled out, the problem of containing them once they occur is increasing in scale and complexity.

Water pollution affects the population at large. For example, mercury gets transmitted via fish, as do many other toxic chemicals. Vegetable plants drawing polluted water yield vegetables that have harmful toxins, and meat of grazing animals also transmits harmful chemicals to human beings. Thus the effects of water pollution can be very complex indeed.

Nuclear Pollution

The emergence of nuclear energy as a 'clean' energy option, especially with the polluting effects of all traditional fossil fuels, gave rise to hopes that this could at last provide an answer to the energy–pollution tradeoff. But soon, major issues arose with regard to the safety of nuclear reactors. From the environment point of view, two issues arose: (a) pollution from the disposal of nuclear waste, something that would be an inevitable by-product of nuclear plants; and (b) pollution that would result in the event of a nuclear accident.

Nuclear wastes pose a special problem in that their decay takes place over thousands of years and over this period, they continue to emit highly harmful radiation that is known to cause a variety of ailments including cancer. Many of their effects are unknown. Hence these are to be disposed of in 'safe' thick lead containers that can contain the radiation; these are to be buried deep in the ground. There is always the possibility of seepage from or breaking of these containers and finding suitable resting places for these nuclear phantoms is a nightmare. No community would like to have these and hence in many cases they are disposed of clandestinely, without the knowledge of the community. In some cases, they have been shipped off to poor countries and disposed of there, with the active connivance and cooperation of corrupt politicians.

Nuclear reactors are built to high levels of safety, and are provided multiple 'fail-safe' systems. But, as the recent experience in Japan shows, it is not possible to predict the worst scenario. After all, it took only a combination of an earthquake and tsunami to wreck the nuclear plants whose cooling systems failed, and seawater and underground water were nearly polluted with radiation. The chances of truly disastrous events may be very small but if they do happen, the consequences are unimaginably serious.

ETHICAL RESPONSIBILITIES OF FIRMS

The issues of pollution are to be largely tackled at the policy level by governments, which need to lay down the needed standards of pollution levels permitted. It is also the government's duty to monitor compliance and punish deviants. But this does not mean that firms have no responsibility for actions in this regard.

Needless to say, it is the duty of firms to adhere to the norms laid down and conduct regular internal checks to ensure compliance. But from the ethical point of view, the responsibility of firms extends beyond this.

First, as noted earlier, all environmental standards are, ultimately, somewhat arbitrary. These standards are the *minimal* levels expected; the firm needs to make its own assessment of the levels that may be harmful to the community around it. Standards usually lag behind the technologies available, and these technologies are not necessarily hugely expensive. For example, in the cement industry, scrubbers and other pollution-neutralizing equipment are available, and some companies (such as Ambuja Cements Limited in Gujarat) have achieved near-zero pollution levels. Similarly, treatment processes are available that reduce or eliminate harmful chemicals in water discharges and enable water to be recycled. Adoption of these new technologies implies respect for the rights of others to lead a healthy and pollution-free life.

Second, firms can help the governments in drafting better legislation. This is possible due to the generally superior knowledge of firms regarding the latest anti-pollution measures available in the industry. This would imply sitting with the government, academics, and NGOs in task forces and committees set up to review pollution norms and devising better ways of monitoring pollution.

Third, firms can be *proactive* in being ahead of domestic norms and opting more for international norms. For example, conforming to Euro V norms may be a good idea for car makers in India, even though Indian regulations may require only Euro IV (or Bharat IV). In fact, it may be a good idea to plan for Euro VI norms that are likely to come into effect in 2014. These will, incidentally, enable these firms to compete better in overseas markets.

On the other hand, certain actions of firms fail the ethics tests. One of them, of course, is to disregard the laws and engage in bribery to keep the government at bay. This is, as is known, a widely prevalent practice, as is clear from the irresponsible behaviour of numerous firms in polluting rivers with the active connivance of government inspectors. It seems that the rivers Ganga and Yamuna are now beyond even divine intervention. Firms go a step further in putting down protests by local affected persons with the help of the police, an arm of the government whose laws the firm has broken in the first place, and hired goons. Then there are other well-known tactics such as playing hide-and-seek when inspectors appear, fudging results, and intimidating independent investigators. Then there are the tactics of commissioning 'research' studies seeking to prove that pollution effects, or the pollution itself, are illusory.

The most well-known exposé of the tactics of firms in underplaying the effects of their pollution is Rachel Carson's *The Silent Spring*. Published in 1962, this book dramatically brought out the effects of pesticides in the environment, including on birds (see Box 7.2).

BOX 7.2

The Silent Spring

This book by Rachel Carson was an attempt to dramatically bring out the effects of pesticides on animals, birds, and human beings, especially DDT, which was used to kill mosquitoes. As suggested by its title, the book sought to draw the picture of a bleak spring with no birds singing because they had all vanished. The chemical industry was up in arms against the book and sought to discredit the author. She was portrayed as a 'hysterical woman', unqualified to talk on such subjects. But the book had huge public readership, and the efforts of the companies to silence it only enhanced its reputation. It highlighted the problems coming up due to the development of resistance by mosquitoes, and warned of the need for increasingly strong pesticides. The book also documented

---

in detail how DDT and pesticides find their way into the food chain, affecting the health of humans, birds, and animals. It is the target of criticism even today, with numerous 'revisits' to the thesis in the book. But the fact remains that with increasing use of pesticides, the difficulty of controlling harmful creatures such as mosquitoes has only grown, not diminished.

The effects of some pesticides linger over many years. But due to their vital interests, firms producing these chemicals underplay the harmful effects, cast aspersions on research scientists warning of ill effects, and even prevent research that they fear may not be in their interest. The shrill and orchestrated campaign against the Nobel Prize-winning team, the Intergovernmental Panel on Climate Change led by R.K. Pachauri, is a pointer to the utterly self-centred and unethical tactics adopted by some firms to prevent findings that may threaten their business.

DEPLETION OF RESOURCES

The pollution problem is different from another environmental problem, namely, depletion of natural resources. While the pollution affects the *present* generation, resource depletion affects the *future* generation. This gives rise to one basic question: Does humankind have any responsibility towards the future generations at all?

There is a school of thought which argues that the present generation does not, in fact, have any responsibility to the future generation. Its arguments are many. First, the future generation is not yet born, and as such they have no rights. Only those living have rights, and there is no knowing yet who the future people are, and whether they will in fact need those rights. If there are to be rights, there must be someone to claim them. And if there are no rights involved, there are no responsibilities either. The second is that there is no knowing as to what the future generation desires. They might not need the same resources that we need today. For instance, they may not need oil because newer technologies may develop that may bypass the need for oil and use other sources such as wind or solar power. The evolution of technologies demands both new resources and abandonment of the old.

Perhaps the most telling argument is that there is a tradeoff between the present generation and the future generation. The present generation has its poor who need to have a better standard of living here and now, and even the others have a right to a better life. When there is talk of conserving resources for the future generations, the questions are how much, and at what cost. Take oil, for example. Oil is a fundamental requirement of the present way of life and drastic reduction in its consumption, while conserving oil for the future generations, will lead to a lowering of living standards of not only the rich but also the poor. Land is ultimately limited, and the only way to cater to the ever-growing population is by increasing the productivity of land through various means such as better fertilizers. But these require some resource or other, notably oil. Hence such sacrifice for the future generation for its uncertain needs will involve certain misery for many in the present generation.

An allied question is: If there needs to be conservation for future generations, for how many generations? If, say, hundred generations, each with an increased size of population, are provided for, there can be consumption of only a tiny fraction of any resources that are available now as, for example, the presently known oil reserves. This applies not only to oil but to all reserves. Clearly, making it sustainable for an infinite number of future generations is going to make those living now unsustainable.

It is also good to remember that earlier predictions of sustainability and the likely duration for which present resources would last have been consistently proven wrong. The most comprehensive attempt to project into the future was done in the early 1970s by the Club of Rome, a group of scientists, statisticians, economists, and intellectuals, to develop a computer model that would predict how long, at the *prevalent* rate of consumption, resources would last. This document was titled *Limits to Growth* (1974). Going by these predictions, the resources should have run out long ago and the world should have come to a standstill. But in reality, a static model cannot predict the new developments that could take place, such as discovery of new sources (such as deep ocean layers for oil), development of new technologies, and new methods of conservation. These make a reliable or even approximate estimate of the extent of conservation of resources for future generations very tricky.

ETHICAL RESPONSIBILITIES OF FIRMS

Does this mean that firms can consume as much of the resources as they like and not worry about the efficacy of their use? No. Ultimately, the resources *are* finite, and even if new reserves are found, generally they are costlier to extract. Hence, both at the levels of the individual as well the firm, there is an ethical imperative that helps present as well as future generations to conserve resources and reduce waste. It is shortsighted and unethical to waste resources simply because the cost can be passed on to the consumer. After all, if a rich person purchases water and throws it down the gutter in a parched desert, his behaviour cannot be excused even if he says he can afford it.

Second, there is an obligation to explore new ways to conserve resources through research done, either on its own or in collaboration with other firms. This can be economically beneficial to firms as well, especially when the prices of resources rise. Carbon credits clearly offer a way to make money through conserving resources (see Box 7.3).

BOX 7.3

Carbon Credits and Carbon Trading

'Carbon credits' is a term used to denote a certificate or permit giving the right to emit one tonne of carbon or carbon dioxide equivalent. This is a part of an international effort to reduce greenhouse gas emissions by capping them for each country and allowing surplus countries (that is, those whose emissions are less than their quotas) to sell their credits to those which are in need of additional carbons. Governments, in turn, allot carbon limits to their businesses, and those that can reduce their emissions can get credit (monetary benefits) and those which increase the emissions (such as by setting up a new factory) would need to buy their rights. The system was formalized in the Kyoto Protocol.

In 2007, the total carbon trading was around US$5 billion, and India had a share of US$1 billion. India is a carbon-surplus country, in that it has achieved more than its quota of emission reduction. It has generated some 30 million tonnes of carbon credits and is generating more credits. The trading is done in international exchanges.

Firms can now not only contribute to the reduction in environment pollution for their own sake, but also make money in the process. This is a case of how you can do well by doing something good. ITC Sonar became the first hospitality chain in the world to earn carbon credits.

Source: 'Carbon Credits and how You Can Make Money from it', http://www.rediff.com/ money/2008/feb/05inter1.htm, accessed on June 24, 2011; 'Carbon Credit', http://en.wikipedia.org/ wiki/ Carbon_credit, accessed on June 24, 2011.

Other actions would involve regeneration of at least some resources as, for example, forests that can be regenerated. Paper mills are major users of forest wood, and they can engage in fresh regeneration through planting new trees (this is done, for example, by the ITC Paperboards and Specialty Papers Division, especially its Bhadrachalam unit). Afforestation also leads to regeneration of oxygen in the atmosphere. Recycling to recover resources is another valid approach. HCL Infosystems, for example, is known for its Green Bag Campaign, working with registered recyclers to ensure maximum and proper recycling of waste (*Business India*, June 12, 2011, p. 68). Corporates are using solar power, at least in a small way, to reduce their consumption of non-renewable energy sources. Ingersoll Rand recently launched the Centre for Energy Efficiency and Sustainability, a think tank of global experts. This body works for 'green operational excellence', in the areas of products and services in different fields such as education, product standards, and communication and trains others to improve their performance in these areas (*Business India*, June 12, 2011, p. 68).

Depletion of resources can affect the present generation also. In Chapter 1, I examined the problems Coca-Cola created for the people in the locality when it chose to situate its water-guzzling plant in a parched location. Depletion of forests by illegal felling of timber, leading often to floods, landslides, and other ecological disasters, unsound and overextensive mining, etc. are distressingly regular happenings, with or without connivance from the government.

Sadly, firms often get away with such behaviour. But once in a while they face popular agitation and action by litigants and the government; such agitation seems to be increasing in frequency and violence. The usual response of firms is to ignore protests or use litigation to stall or curb such activities. But at times firms lose, with major consequences, as happened to Mavoor Rayons Limited, Mavoor, near Calicut (Kozhikode), Kerala (see Box 7.4).

BOX 7.4

The Mavoor Rayons Closure

Mavoor is a relatively unknown town in Kerala, near Kozhikode. In the 1960s, the Aditya Birla Group set up a rayon unit under its Grasim Industries to produce pulp and fibre. Almost from the beginning, the factory faced protests from the community due to the pollution it was causing, notably in the river Chaliyar, into which it allegedly discharged effluents. The management avoided the use of any pollution measures, citing profitability reasons. There was intense agitation and the workers themselves joined the community in a strike. In 1985, the factory was shut down for three years, and it was reported that the damage caused by the loss of employment was significant. The government offered some concessions to the company and it was reopened in 1988.

But the protests continued. The factory was not doing well due to the increased cost of raw materials. In 1999, there was a gas leak that led to the hospitalization of ten persons, and the Kerala State Pollution Control Board ordered its closure pending investigation. In 2002, it was closed permanently, and about 3000 people lost their jobs.

Source: 'Mavoor, http://en.wikipedia.org/wiki/Mavoor, accessed on June 24, 2011.

CONCLUSION

I am not arguing that corporations should abandon their duties towards their shareholders. After all, no one would ask in a shareholder meeting what steps the company has taken for pollution control; all they would want to know is the growth, profitability, etc. the company has achieved. Besides, in an intensely competitive scenario, by going beyond the base requirements of legal compliance (rather than staying well below, if it can get away with it) the firm would be increasing the costs of production and could become uncompetitive vis-à-vis its competitors.

But this point of view fails both the tests of ethics and justice. As we shall argue in Chapter 8, a firm does not exist in isolation; it is in a community. By not caring what damage it causes to the community, whether by pollution or resource depletion it lays its doors open to protests and pressures from society and environmental groups. The more literate and aware a society gets, the greater is its ability to exert such pressure. Ultimately, whatever the 'shareholder value' justification, if a firm poisons the water sources or degrades the soil, deprives many of their livelihood, and spreads diseases in its neighbourhood for maximizing its profits, it has no justification to exist. After all, the executives of the very same firms will not tolerate it if their neighbours throw their rubbish in their compounds or poison their water!

It can be argued that if there are industries, *some* pollution is inevitable. This may be so in many cases, but what is an acceptable level of pollution in terms of acceptability needs to be determined. It depends on the context: drawing water in a region abundant in water is not the same thing as drawing water in a parched desert. The legal limits may set not the *maximum* level that needs to be attained, but rather set the *minimum* levels permissible, and there is a responsibility for a firm to decide how far it can improve on the limit.

Here is the crux of the ethical view. It does not ask whether the firm has complied with the legal provisions (it is expected to do this anyway); it rather asks whether, in the process of utilizing its rights to do business, it does not trample upon the rights of others to exist. It asks not only whether its executives and shareholders are economically better off than before the firm set up shop, but it also whether the community, at least what is near its vicinity, is better off, or at least ensure that it is not worse off.

What Should You, as an Ethical Manager, Do?

The above discussion does not seek to be a one-sided pulpit talk about the virtues of being good regard to environment and its issues. As an ethical manager, you need to recognize the tradeoffs between the firm and its environment, between the present and the future, and between present-day prosperity and sustained existence.

Unfortunately, rewards for managers tend to be based on short-term results. This is especially so in 'professionally managed' firms, driven by quarterly earnings and Dalal Street evaluations, as compared to 'family firms' which can, and often do, take a longer-term view. Perhaps this is because the person likely to run the firm is from the succeeding generations of the family and it is relatively clear who a company's 'professional' successors would be. But managers in the long run are evaluated by the society at large based on a long-term view of their performance, whether they are the 'here-and-now' types or 'today-plus-tomorrow' types.

KEY TAKEAWAYS

1. There is a high degree of awareness about the consequences of different types of pollution and the need to control them.

2. Depletion of resources is an allied but different problem and it affects the sustainability of an organization.

3. Firms can contribute in many ways in the overall effort to control pollution.

4. There are both punitive (through legislation) and reward-based (carbon credits, afforestation credits, etc.) mechanisms to encourage firms to address the problem of environmental degradation due to their activities.

5. A corporation which blatantly ignores the consequences of its actions on the environment and the society around it would lose community support, which it would need when things go wrong.

6. As in all issues of ethics, including personal ethics, a purely consequentialist or utilitarian view can take you only thus far. It is a choice, that you have to make, as to what you want to be.

REFERENCES

'An Inconvenient Truth'. http://en.wikipedia.org/wiki/ An_Inconvenient_Truth, accessed on June 24, 2011.

'Green Economy'. 2011. *Business India*, June 12.

Carson, R. 1962. *Silent Spring*. Boston: Houghton Mifflin Company.

'Carbon Credits and How You Can Make Money from It'. http://www.rediff.com/money/2008/feb/05inter1.htm, accessed on June 24, 2011.

'Carbon Credit'. http://en.wikipedia.org/wiki/Carbon_credit, accessed on June 24, 2011.

Gore, A. (dir.). 2006. *An Inconvenient Truth*. (A documentary film)

'Mavoor'. http://en.wikipedia.org/wiki/Mavoor, accessed on June 24, 2011.

Meadows, D. H. 1974. *Limits to Growth: A Report for the Club of Rome's Project on the Predicament of Mankind*. New York: Signet Books.

8

Business, Community, Society, and Shareholders

'There is nothing so practical as a good theory.'

—Kurt Lewin

'There is nothing so dangerous as a bad theory.'

—Sumantra Ghoshal

From a purely economic viewpoint, firms are economic entities discharging a purely economic function, with little to do with their surrounding community or the society at large, except, of course, for such economic exchanges as they may engage in. Viewed in this way, there are no 'responsibilities' for firms except producing economic value for their shareholders. There are certainly no ethical responsibilities, only legal obligations. To quote Milton Friedman again, the sole social responsibility of a firm is to increase its profits. While it is obliged to observe all the laws, it need not have any concern about the community it is working in, or the society at large. A corporation is totally amoral.

I shall examine the extent to which such a view is valid. Does a firm have what are called 'social responsibilities'? Does it have any ethical responsibilities to the community around it, and to the society at large? What is meant by social or ethical responsibilities for a corporation which is a non-person, only a legal entity? Does the discharge of social responsibilities imply a sacrifice of responsibilities towards its shareholders?

I shall take up these questions using Figure 8.1. It has, first, two concentric circles, the inner circle being the community in the vicinity of the firm, and the outer circle representing the larger society with which it has less direct interaction. Finally, there are the firm's shareholders (who also may form a part of the community and certainly of the society).

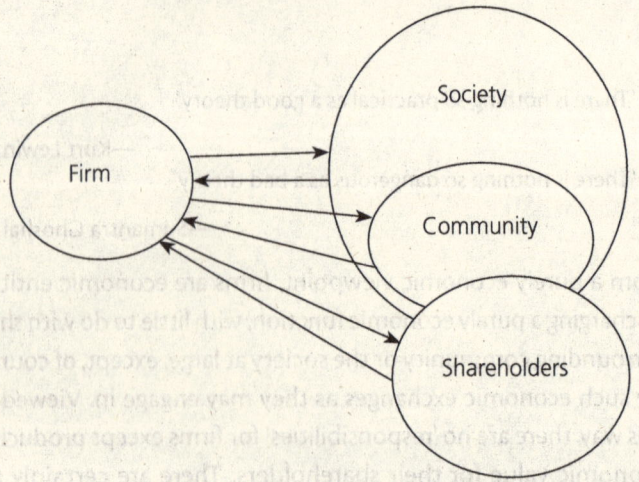

Figure 8.1: The Firm, the Community, the Society, and the Shareholders

THE FIRM AND ITS COMMUNITY

The firm exists in a community. It is expected to play a positive role in improving the quality of life of its community; it certainly has an obligation to see that this community is at least not worse off with the firm as part of it. One set of consequential responsibilities, on the firm and its environment, was discussed in Chapter 7. The firm has an obligation not to damage its environment, air, water, grazing lands, etc. on which the community depends for its existence or quality of life. Polluting water sources or the air infringes on the rights of others to have access to these resources, and hence is clearly unethical. This is especially so since the executives of the firm may not live in that area and hence may not be affected by them.

Usually, but not necessarily, establishment of an industry leads to some immediate benefits to the community in its vicinity. It might provide employment to many people in the community, thus enhancing their income levels. It may provide some new facilities such as hospitals and schools which the community may take advantage of. It might spur the growth of other industries and business opportunities, which again raises the income levels and living standards of the community. In many cases, establishment of an industry may result in an appreciation of land prices which at least some members of the community can take advantage of. But these advantages are accompanied by many negative effects. Thus, in the case of polluting industries such as paper, rayon, or molasses factories, the stench emitted could extend for miles, and the quality of life would take a turn for the worse. The levels of pollutions may rise, taking a toll on life expectancy. As a result, the quality of life may deteriorate; property prices, instead of rising, may crash. Setting up a nuclear plant may also lead to a similar result, and indeed may lead to an exodus from the community. Of course, the firm is not responsible for the property prices or who stays in the vicinity, but it does have a responsibility to see that its actions do not lead to deterioration in quality of life or direct erosion in value of the assets of the community. The interaction of the firm with the community starts right at the time land is to be acquired.

THE PROBLEM OF LAND ACQUISITION

A vexing issue that has come up recently is the acquisition of land for industry. The problem in India arises fundamentally because many people depend on land for their sustenance. Displacing them involves paying them suitable compensation and giving them an opportunity to rehabilitate, and this is usually difficult. Problems arise also from the absence of proper laws for land acquisition and the absence of certainty with regard to the titles for the land. Even for setting up a modest industrial establishment, a sizeable area is required and the industry has to get possession of it or at least needs to have a leasing right over it. Land in India is highly fragmented and as numerous families possess small pieces of land, it is necessary to negotiate with each. Anyone can hold up the process of acquisition, and he knows that the more the land that is already acquired from others, the more is the value of the remaining land that is held up. Thus even though, from an ethical point of view, property rights of each must be respected, this becomes an impossible task in practice.

One way out is to bring in the state as an agency to procure land on behalf of the company. The state has the power to acquire land for a public purpose, and then to sell or lease the land to a company. This way, the company can distance itself from the ethical issues involved in such acquisition. This was what was tried by Tata Motors for land for its proposed Nano facility in Singur. But the acquisition of land was met with opposition from the farmers who felt they were underpaid and the issue became political, leading to violent agitation and loss of life due to police firing. Eventually Tata had to shift out of Singur after having invested some funds there (see Box 8.1).

BOX 8.1

The Not-so Nano Singur Agitation

The state of West Bengal was once the epicentre of Indian industry, with many well-known companies having their production facilities there. In the 1960s, due to the Naxalite agitation and the formation of a communist government that supported violent agitations against management personnel, industry began to shift out, and by the end of the century, the state had lost most of its industries. The image of the state also took a beating. In the mid-decade of the new century, the communist government took a different view and made efforts to attract industry. One firm that responded to these overtures was Tata, which was looking for a site to locate the production facilities for its newly developed small car, the Nano. A site was offered to the company at Singur. This was in a moderately fertile area where the farmers eked out a living on their tiny pieces of land, as they had done for centuries.

Tata Motors did not engage directly in the process of land acquisition. They left it to the state government. The latter went about the process in a rather clumsy way, trying to browbeat the farmers to surrender their land for what the farmers thought were unfair prices. The land in question was fertile land which would be laid to waste, at least for agricultural purposes, and the farmers knew only one occupation: farming. Thus they felt threatened with regard to their future but, ignoring all their objections, 997 acres of land was acquired by the state government in 2006 on behalf of Tata Motors, who started work on their factory. The car was expected to roll out of the factory in 2008. The project would attract an investment of Rs 1000 crore, develop a vendor network, bring in a revenue of Rs 400 crore for the state government, and employment for about 7500 people.

Egged on by political parties, which saw a great opportunity to cash in on the farmers' discontent, the farmers resorted to violent agitations. Many farmers perhaps got good deals, but they were unable to cash in on them. It was alleged that the ruling party brought its own goons to counter those brought in by the opposing parties, and the situation quickly degenerated into a stalemate. In September 2008, Tata Motors at last decided to give up their plans for building a plant at Singur and bore the loss on the investment made thus far. They built another brand new factory in Sanand in Gujarat, which was commissioned in a record time of fourteen months. The first car rolled out in June 2010.

It is not clear who won or lost in this whole episode. Certainly some political parties won a huge advantage in championing the cause of these farmers, and protesting against the state-sponsored violence. The company did not win anything, at least in the short run, although it might have shifted to a state less prone to industrial and social unrest. It still retains the land in Singur. The farmers lost a good opportunity to get good returns on their marginal lands. The state has been seen now as somewhat industry unfriendly and highly unpredictable, so new investments may not be made there readily.

Sources: http://www.merinews.com/article/the-singur-story/125117.shtml, accessed on June 22, 2011; http://www.carblogindia.com/tata-nano-production-started-at-sanand/, accessed on June 22, 2011.

In all fairness, it must be said that Tata Motors did not indulge in unfair or unethical practices in this deal. The agitation was also not directed against Tata as such; it was against the state government which did not take the farmers into confidence during the process of the land acquisition. It had, no doubt, the legal power to acquire the land but the ethical point of view would require it to respect the property rights of the affected farmers and pay them what would be a reasonable price for their land, in addition to giving them an opportunity for rehabilitation. The company was helpless in that it was not dealing with the farmers directly. All the same, the consequences were borne by the company. (The ruling Communist Party lost the elections in May 2011 and the manner it dealt with Singur and similar issues—as for example, at Nandigram—is thought to be a factor that contributed to its defeat.)

Operation of industries generally leads to some deterioration in the quality of life of the community in the form of pollution of the air and water resources, increase in noise levels, degradation of soil, displacement of people, etc., as shown in Chapter 7. The community, of course, also gains in many ways, as I have argued above. Communities generally attempt to get the maximum benefits from the proposed arrival of an industry, and behave opportunistically. But generally things can be negotiated and managed as long as the company's operations lead to a net substantial benefit to the company. The problem comes when a company takes the community for granted and tries to push its way through dubious means.

This approach does not seem to be working in recent years, primarily due to the increased assertion of rights by the community and the volatility of the political climate. But it has to be noted that for every debacle like that in Singur, there have also been cases where there were no agitations, largely due to the way the issues were handled. At the heart of these discussions has been a sense of fairness, justice, and a basic ethical approach.

Some firms have sought to strengthen their links with the communities around them by so-called 'social responsibility' initiatives. I shall return to the theme of social responsibility later in this chapter, but at this point it seems the concept is vague and generally seems to stand for some social initiatives by the company to benefit the community in its vicinity in some way (rather than the society at large). Examples are running of schools (or supporting them), hospitals, and trade-skill enhancement through training programmes. All these, of course, benefit the community, develop the firm's bonding with its community, and help to improve the company's image, although it may be difficult to assess precisely to what extent this increases the company's bottom line.

What Should You, as an Ethical Manager, Do?

It is essential to establish communication with the community at different stages of land acquisition and find common grounds that will be satisfactory to everyone. Land prices are dynamic and no one can say how they will behave once the plant is set up, but at least at the time of starting the acquisition, the price paid must be the fair price; from a practical point of view, a premium may obviate future problems. The test is fairness in dealings.

INDUSTRIAL ACCIDENTS AND THE COMMUNITY

No matter how many precautions a firm takes with regard to its plant and equipment, accidents are bound to occur, and they affect not only the workers in the plant but the wider community as well. This can happen due to different causes: explosion of boiler and high pressure vessels, leakage of chemicals, nuclear accidents, etc. With the increase in chemical industries which also tend to get concentrated in some clusters, the chances of accidents have increased, as have their consequences. Chemical plants usually have toxic chemicals under processing and their leakage (for example, chlorine) can lead to major health problems for the community. Nuclear accidents such as in Chernobyl, Three Mile Island, and now in Japan highlight the huge hazards due to leakage of radioactive compounds that take thousands of years to be neutralized. The most notorious industrial accident, at least for India, is the Bhopal disaster (see Box 8.2).

BOX 8.2

Bhopal: The Unforgettable Disaster

Union Carbide (UC), an American firm, had a subsidiary in India, which operated a pesticide plant in Bhopal, as it does in many countries in the world. Production of most pesticides (which are, by definition, poisonous) involves storage and processing of many toxic chemicals. One such chemical is methyl isocyanate (MIC).

MIC is a liquid chemical which, when it comes in contact with water, produces an exothermic reaction and releases highly poisonous gases. MIC is generally stored in vessels which are connected to the processing plant through valves. At the time of the accident, the particular MIC tank in Bhopal stored 42 tonnes of MIC, much more than that permitted by the company's own safety rules.

On the night of December 2, 1984, at about 10 pm, somehow water entered one of the MIC vessels (there are different theories as to how this happened but I shall not go into them here). Promptly, there was a runaway reaction and quick build-up of pressure, and the gas, mixed with other contaminants resulting from corroded pipes, started escaping into the atmosphere. It

---

rapidly spread into the city and by 2 am, affected people started pouring into the hospitals. The tragedy affected an estimated 100,000–200,000 people; they experienced a number of health problems, notably with their eyes and breathing.

The Indian subsidiary of UC was stated to be functioning independently, although it seems that many of its decisions were controlled by the US Corporate. Of special importance was the conscious non-installation of adequate safety equipment which were routine in UC's own plants in other countries, and the improper maintenance of those which were installed. For example, there was only one backup system for MIC tanks in Bhopal, compared to four that were the norm in US plants. The reduction in the number of backup systems was reportedly done in the case of the Indian subsidiary to reduce the capital costs of the plant. The refrigeration system for the MIC tank was left non-functioning, allegedly to reduce costs. The flare tower and the scrubber were out of service for some time before the incident. There was not enough water pressure on the scrubbing system, and this was a major contributory factor leading to the tragedy (MIC gas is soluble in water and hence, if adequately sprayed with water, much of the gas escaping could have been just washed down).

Besides, there had been moves to reduce staff and the number of people available in the factory was much less than what was needed. The maintenance had, in particular, been pruned to reduce costs. Leaky and corroded pipes were not replaced on time and improper materials were used to cut costs. Employee training was also heavily cut, hence many of the workers had no idea as to what to do in the case of an emergency. There had been a number of incidents involving MIC and other chemicals, and warnings had been sounded by UC's own engineers on the possibility of a runaway reaction; these were ignored.

Warren Anderson, Chief Executive, UC Corporate, did come to Bhopal but fearing massive public outrage was arrested, released on bail, and flown on a special government plane to safety. He returned to the US quickly, and when summoned later to appear before the Indian courts, refused to do so; in effect, he jumped bail. To add to the irony, on December 14, 1984, he appeared before the US Congress and stressed the company's 'commitment to safety'.

The company washed off its responsibility saying the incident occurred due to a disgruntled employee sabotaging the company by deliberately introducing water into the MIC tank. But no employee was ever identified by the company and even if it had been an employee, the company had the constructive responsibility for the actions of its employees. It did not accept any responsibility and did not compensate the victims adequately. The government took it upon itself to be the agency to identify the victims and litigate on their behalf, and it proved to be extraordinarily inept in doing this. There was a settlement of US$475 million from UC, a sum widely perceived to be grossly inadequate. UC shook off all further responsibility, thus effectively saddling the Indian government with the cost of treatment and rehabilitation of the victims. It would seem that what the government did was also grossly inadequate for the numerous victims, many of whom have found peace in death in the intervening twenty-five years.

In 2010, seven Indian (former) employees of UC India were accused of causing death due to negligence and were sentenced to two years of imprisonment. This included the chairman and managing director of the company. They were, however, let out on bail immediately after the verdict. None of the US executives went through any unpleasantness. Anderson is reported to be leading an affluent retired life in the US.

UC itself was taken over by Dow Chemicals which refused to accept any responsibility.

Sources: http://en.wikipedia.org/wiki/Bhopal_disaster, accessed on June 23, 2011; Paul Shrivastava, *Managing Industrial Crisis: Lessons of Bhopal*, New Delhi: Vision Books, 1987.

What Should You, as an Ethical Manager, Do?

The firm has an obligation to see that important safety equipment is installed and functioning. Not doing so, in the interest of shareholder value maximization, can hardly be justified by any sane person. Much of the safety equipment in plants (even fire extinguishers) is kept there with the hope that it will never be used. This leads to the neglect of its maintenance so that when it is actually needed, it does not function. The firm needs to have regular procedures for making sure that all its safety equipment functions properly. Some of this equipment is meant to take care of 'black swan' events, that is, events that are very improbable but can have devastating consequences if they do take place. They usually affect the community in a significant way. Installation of adequate equipment to take care of such eventualities is essential. Finally, industrial accidents would always occur, and the company needs to take its share of responsibility for the damages caused.

ETHICAL TREATMENT OF ANIMALS

When talking about the community and society, usually not much thought is expended towards animals. Do they have any rights? Do firms have any ethical responsibilities towards them?

There are laws in most countries for prevention of cruelty to animals. But cruelty to animals continues unabated, in horrific forms, both in the developing and developed worlds. For example, in most countries, animals to be slaughtered are kept in terrible conditions and painful methods of killing are inflicted on them. In India, their last journey to the abattoir is usually worse than the killing itself. Cows are injected with drugs that produce pains similar to labour pains to make them yield more milk. Some animals are skinned alive to get better leather.

Here, I look at an issue that actually involves an ethical dilemma: the use of animals in clinical research. Newly developed medicines are to be tested and they obviously cannot be tested on humans. So they are tested on various animals such as rats, monkeys, and pigs. The animals are kept in captivity, often in tiny cages with hardly any freedom to move. In many cases they suffer great pain during the experiments, but the dilemma is that, as of now, many of these trials seem to be needed (not necessarily in the same form) before these drugs are administered on human beings as tested drugs. These drugs, of course, could save large numbers of human lives and reduce considerable suffering, and the suffering of some animals may seem to be a painful necessity.

What Should You, as an Ethical Manager, Do?

There are new methods being developed that can obviate the need for animal testing, and even during testing, reduce pain. Your firm can collaborate in such research and adopt its own code of ethical practices for treatment of animals.

Another grey area is the field of clinical testing of drugs. Once drugs are cleared from animal testing, they need to be tested on human beings for their efficacy. This is also inevitable, at least as of now. But the problem is the alleged practices of multinational firms in using people in poor countries for their trials. It is alleged that firms collude with hospitals and doctors to get the number of patients needed to make the results acceptable. But the patients may or may not be paid anything for undergoing these trials and, what is worse, they are often not even informed. When mishaps occur they are covered up; when side effects appear, they are attributed to other factors.

What Should You, as an Ethical Manager, Do?

Managers in collaboration with hospital administrators need to ensure that, at the very least, patients under their charge are told clearly that they are undergoing such trials, and that the company will bear not only the cost of the trials themselves, but also the cost of treatment of any side effects. Clandestine trials definitely do not pass the ethical test. Patients also need to partake in the monetary benefits of the trials enjoyed by hospitals and doctors in an equitable manner.

THE COMPANY, SOCIETY, AND ITS SHAREHOLDERS

By 'society' I mean the larger set of people who are affected by the firm and its actions, beyond the community in the vicinity. While the community is affected *directly* by the firm, society is usually affected only *indirectly*; many of the members of the so-called society may never see the firm or its executives at all. I exclude also the shareholders from this definition of society, for although they, like the community, are part of the external society, they are directly affected by the firm and its actions.

A firm is undoubtedly an economic entity. It is neither an administrative body like the arms of the government nor a social welfare organization. It is set up and exists to give an adequate return on the investment made in it by its shareholders. The shareholders are, in other words, its 'owners', and the managers are employed by these owners to secure for them the best returns on their investment.

This, in a nutshell, is the argument of the so-called Agency Theory (see Box 7.3). It is to be noted that this is not a theory at all; it is just an assumption. But based on this so-called theory, scholars have developed a whole set of arguments that have affected management thinking and practice.

BOX 8.3

Agency Theory: Its Contents and its Discontents

'Agency Theory' found its voice in a much cited paper by M. Jensen and W. Meckling, published in 1976. In this so-called theory, the shareholders were seen as the true 'owners' of the firm which is managed on their behalf by the managers, who thus become their agents (hence the name, Agency Theory). The shareholders' mandate to the managers, in fact the *only* mandate, is to maximize their returns. Hence the sole duty of the managers is to their shareholders, and that duty is to maximize the profit of the firm.

The shareholders' interests may be at variance with those of the managers, who may be interested in maximizing *their own* wealth. So there needs to be put in place a mechanism by which oversight is exercised on managers on behalf of the shareholders. This mechanism is supposed to be the board of directors. The board's function is to exercise supervision on the CEO and the managers and to devise incentives such that the interests of the shareholders and the managers are aligned.

A way to do this was by stock options. The better a company's stock performs, the better the returns to the shareholders, and this prosperity is shared with the managers. Hence, the managers need less supervision. Often, to compensate themselves for doing all this on behalf of the shareholders, the members of the board award themselves stock options or a percentage of the firm's profits.

This ignores the basic point that in firms, value is created not only by the shareholders' capital, but also by the labour of the employees, the knowledge and goodwill generated by the firm, the often subsidized contributions by the state, and those of the society. Now, with the increasing role knowledge plays, knowledge itself is becoming an important factor of production. But agency theorists argue that the shareholders are supreme because the maximum risk is taken by the shareholders, and hence the ownership of the firm is rightfully theirs. But as S. Ghoshal has argued (2005), the shareholders take the *least* risk; the employees take a far greater risk in comprising the firm, and the society bears the cost of the externalities. After all, it is far easier to dispose of a stock than to find a new job.

It has been realized that some of the recent scandals such as with Enron, Global Crossing, etc. arose precisely because of these attempts at the alignment of incentives. There was every incentive for the members of boards and the top management to grant themselves liberal stock options, and take action to inflate the share prices for maximum benefit. The shareholders would obviously be happy to see their wealth increasing, but while managers can use their inside information as to how the company is faring and sell their shares at an opportune moment, the shareholders cannot. By the time the curtain is down, the executives are immensely rich and many shareholders have lost all their wealth (as happened especially with Enron).

When Agency Theory talks about shareholders, it assumes a degree of homogeneity among them. This may not always be the case. The interests of different shareholder groups could be very different as, for example, promoters, institutions, and minority shareholders. This is, in fact, the main concern of corporate governance in India. Agency Theory cannot address this problem at all.

Agency Theory also gives a wrong notion to students and practitioners as to what business is all about. Without understanding the broader issues they start with the notion of profit maximization as the word of the gospel and proceed to act accordingly. This distorts the perception of business by society and leads managers to take blatantly unethical actions, justifying themselves by saying, 'We did all this for you!'

Sources: M. Jensen and W. Meckling, 'Theory of the Firm: Managerial Behaviour, Agency Costs and Ownership Structure', *Journal of Financial Economics*, 3: 305–60, 1976; S. Ghoshal, 'Bad Management Theories are Destroying Good Management Practices', *Academy of Management Learning & Education*, 4 (1): 75–91, 2005.

Milton Friedman's article titled 'The Social Responsibility of a Business Is to Increase Its Profits' in *The New York Times Magazine* (1970) has been quoted, misquoted, and argued over an innumerable number of times. His argument elaborated on the basic idea discussed above: that being mere agents of shareholders, managers have the *sole duty* to increase their wealth, and hence any diversion of the firm's resources to any of the so-called social responsibility activities amounts to putting others' money into uses it was not intended for. This, in fact, is irresponsibility, not responsibility. If the firm is owned entirely by its management, they can do what they want to do with it, but if the firm is a public company, the managers should not put its resources into any activities other than what they were intended for: the pursuit of profit. The firm and its managers simply do not have the mandate to do anything else.

This argument has been attacked by other scholars on different counts. First, it seeks to completely ignore any ethical obligations on the part of a firm; the managers need to worry only about their legal obligations. In other words, so long as they stay within the law, they need not worry about any other impact their actions may have on their stakeholders other than the shareholders. Going one step further, the implication of this approach is that as long as the managers stay within the law, *anything* is not only permitted, but *obligatory* on their part.

This would lead to monstrous malpractices by the companies. Are they *obliged* to indulge in bribing and corruption on behalf of their shareholders so long as they are not caught? If being 'legal' is interpreted as meaning securing favourable judgements on issues, would they be not only permitted but obliged, as their shareholders' agents, to bribe the legal system itself to secure favourable judgements?

Second, it is not clear that the shareholders have in fact given such a mandate to the management as suggested by Agency Theory. They might have invested purely with a speculative motive and many have no stake in the firm as such, only in its current share price. If they feel that they are unhappy with the management, they can always sell their shares and exit. In fact, some surveys carried out on shareholders in the US revealed that the majority *did not* want pure maximization of profits by the firms to the exclusion of all other considerations.

It has been argued by Agency theorists that shareholders are not merely investors; they bear the highest risk. The managers, bound by their contracts, probably bear the least risk in case the firm does not perform well; they can simply join another firm. The secured debt holders can claim the first charge of assets of the firm, followed by the unsecured debt holders, and last, by the equity shareholders, who have to satisfy themselves with whatever is left over after the others claim their dues. The shareholders bear the maximum risk and hence must be rewarded the maximum.

But the opponents of Agency Theory argue that in fact shareholders bear the least risk: they can simply sell off their shares with minimal damage to themselves. The managers generally know beforehand that their firm is in trouble and can quit. It is the workers and the community that bear the biggest brunt in the event of closure of a company. Many workers lose their livelihood and even their entitlements after having worked in the firm; the community might experience other consequences resulting from sudden unemployment after a firm is closed.

The third and most important argument is that even if it is accepted that maximizing shareholder value is the mandate of managers, this maximization needs to be over a *long term*. This is achieved only by adopting sustainable practices and the developing a long-term relationship with stakeholders and the community. No one, of course, can predict what precisely would be the impact of such 'social responsibility' actions on profits, but it would seem that managers taking such corporate social responsibility (CSR) initiatives at least would not have to feel guilty in doing so!

One last argument in favour of CSR initiatives is that the firm does not function entirely as an economic entity anyway, paying fully for all its costs. For example, in many cases, firms are offered land free or at subsidized rates; in most cases inputs such as water are not charged (even if the firm may be in the business of reselling

the water after bottling it with or without adding carbon dioxide!),
the cost of security provided to the company may be virtually nil
or a fraction of what it costs the government, and certain taxes
could be at concessional rates. Thus the cost of what the firm
produces may not truly reflect the costs that actually go into the
product. The argument sometimes advanced is that firms paying
taxes to the government have not much merit in them, since even
individuals who earn pay taxes anyway.

Thus, it seems that there is an obligation for a firm to give back
a portion of its earnings to the society and community. This is not
spending the shareholders' money; rather, it is what enables the
shareholders to earn money in the first place.

A final question to be asked is whether it is the job of a firm to
take up the usual CSR activities such as health and education
services that are the legitimate domains of the government. There
is no doubt that these are indeed tasks that *ought to be* carried
out by the government but in countries such as India, the
government often fails in its duty to deliver these services even
to a modest degree of efficiency, and firms stepping in to fill this
vacuum may be welcome. Even in developed economies such as
the US, governments do not discharge these duties *adequately*,
and there may be areas that can extend beyond what need to be
offered by the government as an obligation. Thus there is a place
for CSR even in developed economies.

It is interesting to note that, no matter what scholars and
academicians may say, practising managers in firms find it perfectly
legitimate and useful to engage in CSR, setting apart a portion of
their firms' earnings. I have not heard of shareholders protesting
against these, though they may have many other grouses against
the management. Hence most major companies have their CSR
programmes. Box 8.4 gives an idea of CSR initiatives taken by some
companies in India.

BOX 8.4

Examples of CSR Initiatives by Indian Firms

Tata Steel was set up in a place called Saatchi, which was in the middle of a jungle, and hence it became imperative to have a township nearby where the employees could live. But the legendary visionary founder, J.N. Tata, visualized not just a township but an ideal township which would have all the facilities of a good town. Thus it was planned with good roads, shady boulevards with blooming trees, hospitals, schools, recreation centres, parks, and markets, all to be administered by Tata Steel itself. The services were free for the employees and were accessible to the others who came to settle in that town, later renamed Jamshedpur. The town is managed by Tata Steel even today and it incurs considerable costs on this account, which ultimately reflects on the cost of its steel. But it has developed strong community and public support which must have stood it in good stead when it needed to expand and to have its iron ore mine lease extended. It has also maintained its competitive position globally, despite the 'unwarranted social costs' it incurs.

Another major steel producing company, JSW Steel, has its plant in Vidyanagar in Bellary District of Andhra Pradesh. Through an independent trust, JSW Foundation, it runs a school and a modest hospital which gives free or concessional treatment to the members of the community in the area (that is, non-employees of JSW). It runs a skill enhancement centre where community children can attend classes to enhance their IT skills and acquire skills required for call centres. Many have been able to get good jobs thanks to this vocational education.

Saint Gobain Glass, Chennai, runs a number of trauma centres to attend to victims of accidents on highways (the factory is located on the Chennai–Bangalore highway). It works in conjunction with the state health authorities to ensure speedy attention to trauma victims. It also supports a number of schools in the vicinity.

Wipro has the Wipro Cares programme which is active in many fields such as education, health, environment, and disaster rehabilitation. Through this programme, Wipro-ites contribute some funds which are matched by Wipro. The employees also volunteer time and effort for selected causes. As part of the programme there are, for example, education projects to help deprived children and provide them with education, and to help girls to complete their schooling. Its Sanjeevani project aims to provide primary health services to the rural community around Wipro's facilities. It has some projects to enhance the quality of the environment as well, with measures such as planting of trees, improving the water supply and the bio-ecosystem.

Jet Airways runs a programme called The Magic Box to help underprivileged children. Though the main source of fund generation seems to be through voluntary donations from the passengers themselves, it administers the fund and organizes, at its cost, special events for children, including organizing free fun rides.

Sources: R.M. Lala, *Creation of Wealth (3rd Edn)*. New Delhi: Penguin Viking, 2004; http://www.wipro.org/community/wipro_cares.htm, accessed on August 3, 2011; http://www.jsw.in/beyond_business/about_foundation.shtml, accessed on August 3, 2011; http://www.jetairways.com/EN/IN/AboutUs/Community Services.aspx, accessed on August 3, 2011, and the personal knowledge of the author.

CAN FIRMS SHAPE ATTITUDES IN SOCIETY?

The traditional view of marketing is that it is a response to the demand that exists in the minds of consumers. This may be too passive a view. As discussed in Chapter 4, firms actively *create* demand through a variety of ways, notably advertisements. When advertisements are directed towards positive objectives, they serve a social purpose. But when they encourage and glamourize harmful substances or habits as, for example, cigarettes or smoking, or create a subtly negative attitude towards some practices such as breastfeeding, then they are definitely not being socially responsible or ethical. Children are tempted in a variety of ways— by junk food, sugar-rich drinks, expensive toys, gadgets, etc.—and the result is obesity, loss of health, accidents, and perhaps a wrong attitude towards life. These are significant—at times huge— negative externalities.

A more subtle effect is the way attitudes are shaped through advertisements. I had pointed out the way fairness creams created a certain attitude towards being dark in complexion. Advertisements showing overaggressive and even callous behaviour—such as driving at high speed through city roads with a girlfriend—glamourize such behaviour, which is often emulated by children.

Media firms contribute their bit. Television serials depicting certain types of behaviour—such as that of mother-in-law to daughter-in-law, macho behaviour by husbands, criminal acts as glamourized actions, and so on lead to promotion of such behaviour, especially among children. Violence on screen and television, it has been found in many studies, promotes violence in children and adolescents who become immune to violence and can commit horrific acts of cruelty without the slightest twinge of conscience. Clearly, such shows do not do much good to society as a whole.

Ethical responsibility arises from the fact that firms have so much choice in most of these matters. As noted in Chapter 6, firms can be more truthful in advertisements, can avoid stopping research programmes seeking to investigate the effects of their products, and avoid themes known to cause undesirable results.

It is sometimes argued that in a free market and society, firms have the right to market products that they find are profitable (that is, they can maximize the profits for their shareholders), and the customers have the freedom to choose. The former is not an absolute right but is contingent on the rights of others to lead a good life, and the right not to be misled by powerful and persuasive communication. The so-called freedom of choice is not as real as it appears on the surface: attitudes, values, and behaviour are the products not only of 'objective' experiences and information, but also of highly subjective and manipulated experiences and information. Firms indulging in such manipulation know full well what they are doing and inasmuch as they are thus indulging in deception, their behaviour deviates from the standards of ethics.

SHAREHOLDERS AND SOCIETY: ARE THEIR INTERESTS IRRECONCILABLE?

With regard to Agency Theory and the responsibility to shareholders, I pose a question: Is the responsibility towards shareholders and towards the larger society as incompatible as is often made out? In other words, does recognizing the responsibility towards the community necessarily imply that the cost of this is to be borne by the shareholders? If a firm spends money on, say, pollution control instead of just dumping its effluents into the rivers, or if it spends money on CSR initiatives, are its managers shortchanging its shareholders, thus compromising on their primary duty towards its shareholders?

Such a question essentially assumes that this is a zero-sum game: what the society gains is necessarily at the expense of the company's shareholders. This may be a flawed view. If, by keeping good relations with society and scrupulously avoiding any damage to the environment, the long-run profits of corporations could be increased, then the shareholders also stand to benefit by these measures. It is unwise to confuse shareholder value with *short-term* shareholder value.

The amount spent on CSR activities is usually small, certainly much less than that spent on advertising. And, as in the case of advertisements, there is no knowing whether it is a waste or an essential part of business activity. The community and society's support leading, in the long run, to better financial performance is as much an assumption as is the shareholders wanting *nothing but* the maximization of their return.

It could be argued that though the amount spent on CSR, community relationship building, and even being ethical may not be very high, it has to be seen in relation to what the competition does. Given the thin margins many firms operate on, even a small additional expenditure can lead to a loss of competitiveness. It has been seen that while everyone wants green instruments or ethical treatment of animals, no one is prepared to pay a higher price for green products. This is partially true. But while the niche for such products may be small, it exists; further, companies could develop a reputation that lead to lowering of other costs such as transactions.

As I shall argue in a later chapter, these matters cannot be argued in terms of costs alone. I am not discussing in this book how to enhance competitiveness, but the issues involved in business ethics. These, in the ultimate analysis, stop at the level of individuals. Individuals have to decide what position they should take with regard to ethics.

CONCLUSION

In this chapter, I have looked at the ethical issues involving a firm with regard to its external stakeholders: the community in which the firm and its factories work, the society it interacts with, and its shareholders. From an ethical point of view it has responsibilities towards all of them, not just to its shareholders. If a corporation is a legal fiction, so is Agency Theory with its argument of the shareholders being the *sole* stakeholders. A corporation draws its capital resources from its shareholders, but it also draws other resources from other stakeholders including its employees (who contribute labour), the government (which gives it security and a regulatory framework to operate in), the community (which sacrifices some quality of life), and society (which gives it legitimacy). The real task of an enlightened management is to strike a balance among all these not necessarily compatible viewpoints and demands.

KEY TAKEAWAYS

1. The firm has an obligation to the community not to deteriorate the environment, to enhance the quality of life and at least to not reduce it.

2. Earlier, firms could get away with blatantly unethical practices with respect to the community. Now, with

increased awareness, this is becoming more and more difficult.

3. The thesis that shareholders form the *only* relevant constituency for a firm does not find wide acceptance today. Other stakeholders are also seen as important.

4. CSR initiatives taken by companies recognize the fact that the firm has a broader link with the community around it.

5. The firm shapes the attitudes in society, and hence it has a responsibility not to shape them in a wrong direction that ultimately leads to enhanced social problems.

6. The so-called contradiction between responsibility to the community/society and shareholders is largely illusory. Managers have to recognize that they have responsibilities to all three, and have to thus strike a balance.

REFERENCES

http://www.merinews.com/article/the-singur-story/125117.shtml, accessed on June 22, 2011.

http://www.carblogindia.com/tata-nano-production-started-at-sanand/, accessed on June 22, 2011.

http://en.wikipedia.org/wiki/Bhopal_disaster, accessed on June 23, 2011.

http://www.wipro.org/community/wipro_cares.htm, accessed on August 3, 2011.

http://www.jsw.in/beyond_business/about_foundation.shtml, accessed on August 3, 2011.

http://www.jetairways.com/EN/IN/AboutUs/CommunityServices.aspx, accessed on August 3, 2011.

Ghoshal, S. 2005. 'Bad Management Theories are Destroying Good Management Practices', *Academy of Management Learning & Education*, 4 (1): 75–91.

Jensen, M. and W. Meckling. 1976. 'Theory of the Firm: Managerial Behaviour, Agency Costs and Ownership Structure', *Journal of Financial Economics*, 3: 305–60.

Lala, R.M. *Creation of Wealth* (3rd Edn) 2004. New Delhi: Penguin Viking.

Shrivastava, P. 1987. *Managing Industrial Crisis: Lessons of Bhopal*. New Delhi: Vision Books.

9

Building an Ethical Organization

'Integrity should be the litmus test for managerial character.'

—Peter Drucker

How do you create an ethical organization—an organization that
discharges its duties towards its shareholders, obeys all the laws
of the country, and is also ethical? Is it reasonable to make such a
demand on an organization?

Of course, *all* organizations claim that they are ethical. They
even put it in their mission statement. But the real test, of course,
is how they react to situations or the kind of situations they create.
As the noted Harvard Business School professor Joseph Badaracco
has pointed out in his book, *Defining Moments: When Managers
Must Choose between Right and Right* (1993), there are no absolutely
ethical or unethical decisions; managers have to choose not
between right and wrong but between right and right, between
wrong and wrong. These are dependent on the personal values
of the managers and cannot be uniform all over the organization.
The implication is that the choices of different managers in a given
situation cannot be uniform. What appears right for one may not
appear so for another. Yet there needs to be an overarching
framework of values for each organization that can be applied to
it, in other words, *a value system* for the organization, as distinct

from that for an individual. For example, an individual may feel that there is nothing wrong in fudging expense accounts as long as these are small, but an organization may explicitly prohibit such behaviour. An employee may be a male chauvinist who feels there is nothing wrong in passing derogatory remarks about women or women employees in particular; company policy may prohibit such comments. But when an outsider (customer, supplier, consultant, or community representative) interacts with an organization, he would need to have some predictability of how different members of an organization would look at a certain issue. These expectations also go to make the value system.

The question then is: how to build an ethical organization that makes clear the expectations it has from its employees regarding ethical behaviour. I propose a three-pronged approach involving (a) the creation of a suitable structure and incentives for ethical behaviour; (b) the creation of an ethical climate and culture within the organization; and (c) the leader playing a role as not just the Chief Executive Officer, but also the Chief Ethical Officer in setting the ethical climate of the organization.

CREATION OF A CONDUCIVE AND ENABLING STRUCTURE AND SYSTEM

People ultimately act based on the incentives for their actions. If ethical behaviour is rewarded, there is a good chance that they will act ethically; if it is not rewarded, or in fact punished, they will probably not act ethically, whatever platitudes the top management makes.

Not that there are no guidelines in organizations delineating ethical behaviour. Usually there are explicit and implicit guidelines, sometimes very detailed ones, but the real issue is how organizations enforce those guidelines. When violations take place, what happens? If an employee says he could not do a certain thing because a guideline prohibits it and there is a negative consequence for the organization, what is the reaction from the ones higher up? These determine how employees *interpret* guidelines and observe them in practice. For example, if an employee is unable to effect a sale because the sale would involve illegal gratification (explicitly prohibited by the company, as happened in the Lockheed scandal), how does the organization handle it? If the contract is won after bribing, how does the company handle *that*? And if the scandal comes out into the open, how does the company handle the situation?

A major reason for unethical behaviour is the way targets are set. Often very difficult targets are set, and not attaining them attracts severe penalties. Employees quickly find ways to cut corners to meet targets. If the company just wants to know whether their targets are met or not and if they have been met, does not want to know how they have been met, the word quickly spreads, and soon everyone is playing the game and cutting corners.

This is the situation Jack Welch of GE warned about. The targets set by him in GE were very stiff and difficult to meet but some did meet them. He noted that there will always be some 'Type-4' managers who would meet the targets but through dubious means (see the case reference given at the end of this chapter). They do not share the organization's values. Removing them is a difficult decision because of their competence and ability to deliver results, but Welch insisted that this be done. These Type-4 managers may take unauthorized shortcuts (for example, showing goods as sold with cooperation from the buyers), creating a harsh climate of working for employees (simply bulldozing them), or engaging in outright illegal practices such as forging documents (as happened in the case of B.F. Goodrich, see Chapter 5). A real danger is that the top management of the organization does not know what is really going on in the organization.

On the other hand, persons with integrity need to be rewarded. Even if some of them may not be star performers, their performance can be improved through training, they can be given positions more suited to their abilities. Their correct attitudes may be an asset for the company in the long run. A crucial reward would be the company's support in the stand taken by such an employee. Supporting such employees gives a powerful signal to the outside world on how seriously the company takes its profession of values.

From an ethical point of view, it may be a good idea to have people challenging company decisions in open meetings, especially on its ethical aspects. In other words, there should be 'devil's advocates' whose task it is to look specifically at the ethical issues in a decision. This is not to be obstructive or with a view to prevent a decision from being taken, but rather to bring to the table the ethical side of issues so that all are aware of them. (In the old days, kings used to have a *vidushak* or court jester who had the liberty to point out the errors the king made, in a comic or humorous way. Besides lightening the court atmosphere, they also served as conscience keepers).

Another structural device would be *ethics committees*, whose job it should be not to give lectures on the importance of ethics, but to investigate cases where ethical norms may have been breached. Many organizations already have committees to investigate gender issues. There could be other committees to investigate customer-related issues, supplier-related issues, and environment-related issues.

Having a sound system of corporate governance would help in bettering the ethical orientation of an organization. Boards play a crucial role in bringing about a better balance between the interests of the shareholders, management, employees, and different sections of the shareholders, especially the minority shareholders. A well-constituted and functioning Board can be a structural mechanism for ethical decision-making.

Boards are not merely supervising bodies to ensure maximization of profits for shareholders; they are charged with the functioning of the firm as a whole in a satisfactory manner. The CEO has to answer to the Board regarding not only purely economic business decisions but also decisions involving ethical angles.

For this to happen, the composition of the Board is crucial. If the same person acts as the chairperson of the Board and the CEO (the position of chairman and managing director, or CMD), the chances of challenge to the CEO's personal value-dominated decisions are reduced. Separation of the Board chairperson and CEO could enhance a creative discourse between the two persons and other members of the Board. But, as is seen in India, most firms are family run, and whether the two positions are combined or separate, effective control lies with the family. Here it becomes important to have independent directors who could feel secure in questioning the CEO's decisions, and, perhaps, through informal interactions, influence the CEO's thinking. In the Indian context, in most firms, independent directors are effectively chosen by the CEO, and hence their true 'independence' is in doubt. But while independent directors can function as friendly critics, their willingness to speak out, especially on matters involving ethics, is enhanced if the CEO makes it clear that they are *expected* to give their independent views, and that their views will be heard.

It is, of course, true that if the CEO wants to be unethical, the independent directors may not be able to stop him. But in many situations, it is not necessarily the case that the CEO *wants* to be unethical, but the issues are not clear. As shown in Chapter 3, it is really a tradeoff between conflicting demands, choices between right and right actions. It is in such situations that independent directors can play a constructive role.

Other Board mechanisms such as the audit committees and appointments committees can play a useful role in bringing to the attention of the Board instances or early signs of fraud. Some of the recent scandals leading to the demise of firms could have been avoided if the audit committees and external auditors had done their job.

Structural mechanisms lay the foundation on which firms can build their ethical superstructure. Ultimately, they specify the rules under which the activities of the firm take place. In a sense, they specify the 'don'ts' rather than the 'dos'. They specify the limits of the playground, but do not tell the players how to play. That is done by the culture of the organization.

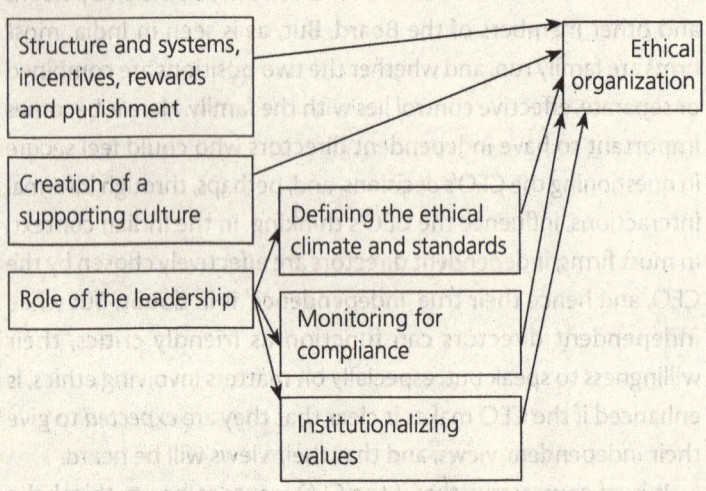

Figure 9.1: Creation of an Ethical Organization

CREATION OF AN ETHICAL CLIMATE AND CULTURE IN THE COMPANY

Structure decides how people *should* behave, but it cannot ensure that they *do* behave in the desired ways. A set of ethical rules that depend solely on rewards and punishments is not likely to succeed. What is needed is the *software*, the patterns of behaviour people *willingly* indulge in. In an ideal situation, these behaviour patterns are so internalized that there is no *need* for any rules and norms, but this is an ideal state, rarely attainable, hence the need for rules and stated norms. But the objective should be to drive towards more of a *willing* compliance.

Consider, for a moment, how a family functions. There are shared and understood patterns of behaviour; everyone *knows* what is acceptable and what is not. Yet there are no written rules; there are only unwritten norms. Of course, in a family, the members are bound much more by emotions; while in organizations, emotions may play a smaller role. All the same, every organization develops its own norms of behaviour, and this forms its culture. This is propagated and continued through shared stories, myths, and informal exchanges between its members. Some culture *always* exists in every organization; the challenge is how to channelize it in the desired direction.

This is achieved through a multiplicity of devices. Invariably, the leader's attitudes and expectations are to be conveyed to the organization members, who act to conform to them, or at least to what they perceive them as. Oral communication is, of course, important, and its effectiveness depends on the sincerity and genuineness of the communication. But much more important are the actions—how the top management responds to situations that do arise.

Aravind Eye Hospitals in Tamil Nadu is a good example of how a climate and culture was consciously created by its founder, Dr Venkataswamy ('Dr V.') and his family members (see Box 9.1). It was a combination of an ideal he presented as a vision, his personal values, the constant but unobtrusive reminder of these values through the pictures of Sri Aurobindo and the Mother in the hospitals, and the examples set by the top management. Among other values, it was made clear that ethical transgressions would never be tolerated. Even after Dr V.'s death in 2006, the hospitals continue to have the same ethical and service values that they started with.

BOX 9.1

Aravind Eye Hospitals

The Aravind Eye Care System, with its main unit in Madurai, Tamil Nadu, has a number of units contributing to eye care. There are five hospitals, the biggest one (and the one it started with) being in Madurai. The first hospital was founded by Dr V. after his retirement from regular service, out of his personal savings. He started this venture with a simple mission: 'Eradication of needless blindness', and this vision continues even today. Much of the blindness in India was (and still is) caused due to cataract, hence he concentrated on this problem. Most of the affected patients are from the poorer sections, and he gave them free treatment. Over the years, the hospital has been doing about 60 percent of its surgeries for *free*, and it introduced highly productive 'assembly line' type of surgeries, enabling each doctor to do about twenty five surgeries per half day (the operation theatres were cleaned and disinfected in the afternoons) as compared to five or six surgeries in other hospitals. This continues to be the norm.

This demands high commitment from the doctors. Dr V.'s team impressed the doctors with the notion that they were not there just to earn a living, but to engage in a noble mission. Dr V. was himself a follower of Sri Aurobindo, the sage from Pondicherry (after whom the hospitals were named), and the pictures of Sri Aurobindo and the Mother were put up everywhere. There were meditation rooms and sessions, again a spiritual reminder of their mission. These can still be seen in the Aravind Eye Hospitals.

A cardinal aspect of Aravind culture is the respect expected to be given to everyone. However poor a patient is, he is seen as an enabler for achieving the mission, and has to be treated with respect. No misbehaviour of any kind is tolerated. Similarly, all staff is treated with respect. News regarding cases of misbehaviour spread quickly, and the person responsible is put under great peer pressure to mend his ways.

Ethical dealings are absolutely vital. The hospitals have never paid bribes. They do not have part-time visiting doctors since they could indulge in malpractices and might not subscribe to the culture of the organization. They do not entertain any recommendation for appointments or for 'priority' treatment.

The hospitals have consistently done extremely well financially also, and despite their giving free treatment to more than half their patients, they do not take any donation or government subsidies. They are internally financially self-sufficient, and have capital for building new facilities. They have also generated tremendous goodwill in the community and in the state of Tamil Nadu, and this goodwill has translated into the chain having very little difficulty in its expansion in Madurai and other cities.

Source: 'Aravind Eye Care System: Giving Them the Most Precious Gift', Case No. BP 0299, Indian Institute of Management, Ahmedabad, 2003.

Power is an essential tool by which executives control those below them. But it is a misconception that power is to be exercised visibly. Studies have shown that the most effective leaders are subtle in their exercise of power. Political scientist James MacGregor Burns concluded that the most effective leaders are those who share their needs, aspirations, and values with their followers. They build deeper connections among organization members, and this becomes the culture of the company.

Actually, institutionalizing an ethical culture, especially in the early stages of an organization, is not all that difficult. Many organizations such as Tata, Infosys, Wipro, Mahindra & Mahindra, and Sankara Nethralaya have successfully instituted a highly ethical culture within their organizations. It depends to a great extent on the leadership, especially the founding leadership. I shall now examine the role leadership plays in setting an ethical climate in an organization.

THE ROLE OF LEADERSHIP

The role of leadership is crucial to the way an organization does its business, , but this is especially so in the case of the ethical climate in the organization. An organization is as ethical as the top management wants it to be. The role of the top management can be seen in three areas: (a) defining the ethical values and standards; (b) monitoring their compliance; and (c) institutionalizing them so that they get passed on to the next generation and become the core values of the organization.

Defining the Ethical Values and Standards

The members of the top management, usually the founders, define the kind of organization they desire. For example, Narayana Murthy and his founding team at Infosys were clear from the beginning that they would not resort to unethical practices in dealing with governments, procuring contracts, dealing with employees, etc. This was discussed and formally agreed upon, and all the founders scrupulously adhered to it. Since paying lip service to ethics was the usual norm in companies in India, they had to demonstrate their seriousness and commitment to these values. This they did through constant reiteration, and showed it in practice by refusing deals that were lucrative but involved compromise. In the 1980s, when the Licence Raj was still in full force, this meant forgoing many opportunities and having only limited growth. The organization opted for this rather than compromising on its values.

Dr V. also defined his core values clearly, and those who joined his hospitals needed to adhere with existing core values. Skill was important, but the right attitude and values were vital for an employee to be recruited and retained.

Over a period of time, these organizations acquired a reputation for their competence as well as ethical standards, and this helped them build their corporate brands. Their reputation—built painstakingly—started paying dividends when they became good companies to work for and started attracting good applications. Infosys became such an attractive employer that the number of job applications it received was beyond the capacity of its HR managers to deal with in the usual way, and more efficient procedures for screening them had to be devised.

It is said that recruitment takes place because of the reputation of a company and separation takes place because of the boss.

Often the problems that arise are due to conflict in values rather than competence mismatch. Bosses, themselves under pressure, demand shortcuts from those working under them, and when the subordinate persons do not agree to take such shortcuts, major problems arise. How these issues are resolved by the management sets the climate in the organization.

Many of the writings on ethics may leave one with the impression that being an ethical organization would lead eventually to success, although the path may be long and arduous. But for every case that is a success, there may be at least one which was unable to fight the system and win. There was a builder in South India who started on the real estate building business insisting that he would not resort to unethical practices, including bribery. The real estate sector is notorious for its low ethical standards and since a large number of clearances are needed from different government agencies, each of which can hold up progress, bribery is extensive and accepted as a part of the cost of doing business. This builder acquired a reputation for his clean dealings, which added a degree of trustworthiness to issues such as land titles. People felt more confident dealing with his company, and it not only acquired a reputation but also commanded a good market share. It seemed there was room for a firm with integrity in the world of builders.

Then the empire struck back. All the tricks in the trade to delay projects and harass the builder were employed. Eventually the builder had to accept defeat and close his business.

Unfortunately, events of this nature are the norm, not the exception. Being ethical involves a great risk for the leader, even at a personal level. As I argue in the next chapter, leaders need to define their own standards not because it is more profitable to do so, but because it is the *right thing* to do.

Monitoring Compliance

The second task of the leader is to ensure that the standards laid down are complied with. There must be some core values, the violation of which cannot be tolerated. Here the individual issues need not come to the top management but should be dealt with within the policy framework. But when cases are outside the usual policy framework or involve senior management personnel, the top management comes into the picture and has to decide on what to do in a particular case. What the management does is watched by the employees and the other stakeholders. Therefore, each decision becomes a defining point for the ethical stance of the organization itself.

For example, suppose there is an allegation of sexual harassment by a senior management personnel located in the USA (as is now the case with many Indian companies). It is a known fact that many employees use the allegation of sexual harassment to harass the boss into giving them undue favours (such as, for instance, a raise or a better performance rating). This is especially so in the USA. But when a complaint is registered with the police or a suit is filed in a court the matter becomes very different, with laws of other countries and perhaps racism being involved. The company has to ensure that justice is done by instituting a fair enquiry so that a chance is given not only to the employee who is alleging such harassment but also the person against whom allegations are made. Sacrificing the senior employee as a measure to avoid a scandal may be as unethical as shielding him.

It has to be recognized that however well intentioned the top management may be and however exemplary its own actions at the ethical level, there are bound to be many violations that may be going on at different levels in the organization. After all, everyone does not share the same values. Sometimes people act believing that they are acting as per the ethical guidelines of the company or, in other words, they interpret the guidelines and act as per their interpretation, but others may not think so. Here it is a case of genuine difference in opinion. On the other hand, there may be other cases where there is no question that the people concerned acted unethically, fully knowing that what they were doing was unethical. Both types of cases need to be monitored and there needs to be a process by which action is taken. In the second type of case, the employee needs to be terminated or (rarely) given a second chance, and be clearly told that a repetition would be unacceptable. In the first case, it could be trickier, involving understanding the employee's point of view. But in both cases there needs to be a mechanism by which the CEO knows what is going on in the organization.

Institutionalizing the Values

This is probably the most difficult of all. How do you ensure that the values are preserved after your term is over, and are passed on to the next generation? In truth, there is really no way to ensure this, but there are ways to make it more *likely* that the desired results are achieved.

It starts with the choice of the successor, which is determined by a variety of factors such as competence, ability to face the particular environment of the company, and values of the successor. Values form only one part of the profile desired in a successor. But this is an important part.

Usually the values of the prospective successor, as applied to the particular requirements of an organization, are not easy to identify, especially if the successor is an outsider. The track record, the way the successor has dealt with ethical issues in the past, and his pronouncements may give vital clues, but still they are just that—that—clues. It is for this reason that bringing in outsiders is always fraught with risk, especially in organizations which pride themselves on their culture and ethical values. Insiders are, by and large, known to everyone in the company, and the risks of a misfit are much less. This is one reason why organizations that lay great emphasis on their culture and values tend to prefer their internal members for the top position. For example, Hindustan Unilever (and its predecessor company, Hindustan Lever) has always had internal succession; so has GE. IBM and 3M have had outsiders only once in their history.

The board can also act as a monitoring mechanism. Usually the CEO and the chairperson of the board do not change together. Thus a certain degree of continuity is ensured and needs to be capitalized on.

Setting up and institutionalizing strong systems is another way of ensuring continuity. Once set up, these systems and operating procedures acquire a life of their own. Checks and balances, for example, ensure that there is no undue concentration of power with anyone, including the CEO. There is no guarantee, of course, that a determined CEO will not change these systems, but having well-institutionalized systems makes their continuity more likely.

The best leaders are not those who become indispensable and who decide and define everything. The creative force of an organization arises from the way the leaders empower their followers and have them willingly follow a common vision and value system. The best system is that in which employees do not merely follow rules but understand why they are following them, and do so willingly, even standing up against their superiors. This is true institutionalization.

These ideas are well brought out on the establishment and institutionalization of values at the Indian Institute of Management, Ahmedabad (IIMA).

BOX 9.2

Building the Indian Institute of Management, Ahmedabad

The framework presented in Figure 9.1 can be used to understand how IIMA, the premier management institution in India, was built.

IIMA was set up as a part of Jawaharlal Nehru's vision to have world-class institutions in India. It was set up in collaboration with Harvard Business School, but it was not named Institute of Business Management. It sought to improve management practices of not only industry, but also the government and NGOs. Thus it defined its vision in terms of its responsibilities to the society and community.

From the beginning, it was agreed that the highest ethical standards would be maintained in every aspect of its working. This was not handed down from the top, but agreed to by all concerned: faculty, officers, and staff. To prevent undue concentration of power with the director, which could lead to dependence on his personal value systems for the Institute to follow, a decentralized system with faculty governance was put in place. Many attempts by the government to interfere for personal gain were frustrated by the stand taken by the Institute. For example, when a Secretary to the Government of India wanted his son to be given 'consideration' for admission, and threatened unpleasant consequences if the admission was not given, the then director simply put it up to the Admissions Committee to give it due 'consideration'. He pleaded helplessness in the face of the decision of the Admissions Committee in such cases. There has never been a case of interference with admission decisions ever since, unlike most other institutions in India, which 'oblige' powerful people in exchange for favours.

The major decisions taken by the Faculty Council rather than by the director or the board has enabled IIMA to withstand pressures to compromise on many aspects as, for example, student evaluation, setting and enforcing standards for compliance by students and faculty and appointment of faculty and staff. The supporting culture that was instituted was one of enablement rather than enforcement.

In nurturing the Institute's values and traditions, the founder, Ravi Mathai, played a decisive role. He was not an academic, but understood how an academic institution is to be run. He let the various committees take their decisions and interfered only when necessary. He was a person with impeccable integrity and served as an ethical role model. He had the ability to stand back and allow the faculty and officers to take the decisions, without finding the need, usually born out of a sense of insecurity, to centralize decision making. But when there were transgressions as, for example, cases of plagiarism, the Institute could step in harshly and require the persons concerned to leave the Institute, even though it always had the problem of faculty shortage. Thus was the function of monitoring of compliance achieved.

Institutionalization was achieved by setting clear norms (rather than detailed written rules) for how to deal with a question; the underlying concept was that of fairness rather than mechanical adherence to rules. It is remarkable that, despite having many directors with widely differing preferences and ideas, the Institute has been able to maintain its systems and traditions to a large extent till today. No scandals have ever been reported although much uninformed criticism continues to emanate periodically. Having such high standards of ethics and a supporting culture has served also to attract quality faculty despite its rather unattractive location (at least as compared to metros). It has also been able to achieve a ranking of eight in the MBA programmes all over the world, and twelve among all the one-year MBAs. Thus ethics has not stood in the way of accomplishment of its primary mission.

Source: Ravi Mathai, et al., *Institution Building: The IIMA Experience. Vol. 1 and Vol. 2.* Ahmedabad: Ravi Mathai Centre for Educational Innovation, Indian Institute of Manangement, Ahmedabad, 1993.

CONCLUSION

Building an ethical organization needs simultaneous building of the structure, the culture and systems, and the leadership. The structural mechanisms provide the hardware, the culture and systems provide the software, and leadership provides the power supply. All are needed to ensure a healthy ethical climate.

But finally, there is no escape from the fact that an organization is only as ethical as its CEO wants it to be. All the structural mechanisms discussed can work only if the CEO and the top management want them to work the way they are supposed to. A number of case studies have been written on Enron and the role played by its top management. On this, as well as in the Satyam scandal, the mechanisms were all there; the board members were well respected and reputed; the audit firms were vintage firms. Yet each one of them was corrupted by a management that gave no regard to ethics whatsoever. Enron's board members had stocks and options worth millions; they had little incentive to raise red flags and quit. In the case of Enron, the audit firm also had a consulting wing that had lucrative consulting assignments with Enron, which clearly set up a conflict of interest. Employees who raised suspicion were ordered to pipe it down and threatened; the boards preferred to look at the paper results put up before them year after year and did not want to see what was going on underneath the figures. Many of the top executives in Enron who knew the true situation sold off their shares before the company crashed and became millionaires. But some of them, notably Kenneth Lay, the CEO, and Jeff Skilling, the CFO, got indicted. Ramalinga Raju, CEO of Satyam, is still in jail (at the time of writing this).

A CEO who wants to build an ethical organization has an excellent chance to do so and can still be successful as a business leader, creating value for his shareholders. But a CEO who does not care about ethics is sure to build an organization that is unethical.

KEY TAKEAWAYS

1. Creating an ethical organization involves three components: creation of the appropriate structure and systems, creation of an appropriate culture, and providing an ethical leadership.

2. The role of leadership consists of three components: (a) defining the ethical values and standards; (b) monitoring compliance; and (c) institutionalizing the values.

3. Structure provides the hardware. Culture provides the software. It is the leadership which is the power supply. An organization can only be as ethical as its leader wants it to be.

4. Of these, institutionalization is the hardest and requires a consistent and persistent push in the early stages of the organization. Leadership plays a vital role in this.

REFERENCES

Badaracco, J. 1997. *Defining Moments: When Managers Must Choose between Right and Right.* Boston: Harvard Business School Press.

Bartlett, C. and M. Wozny. 2004. 'GE's Two-Decade Transformation: Jack Welch's Leadership', Case # 9-399-150. Boston: Harvard Business School.

Manikutty, S. 2003. 'Aravind Eye Care System: Giving Them the Most Precious Gift', Case No. BP 0299. Ahmedabad: Indian Institute of Management.

Mathai, R., *et al.* 1993. *Institution Building: The IIMA Experience. Vol. 1 and Vol. 2.* Ahmedabad: Ravi Mathai Centre for Educational Innovation, Indian Institute of Management, Ahmedabad.

10

On Becoming an Ethical Manager

'It has become dramatically clear that the foundation of corporate integrity is personal integrity.'

—Samuel DiPiazza, CEO, PricewaterhouseCoopers, 2003

Much of what I have discussed thus far pertains to what a manager should do in his role as a manager or an employee. Accepting a role in an organization would involve certain things that are expected from that role, whether or not you like doing them. Many, probably most, employees join an organization not to express their personal values but to carry out certain tasks that their role demands (and get paid for doing so). The employee may (in all probability does) take up a job simply to earn a living and it would be extraordinarily lucky for him if his personal values coincide with those demanded by his job. To cite some extreme examples, a person may detest killing animals, but may, by force of circumstances, join an abattoir; another might become an executioner, though the last thing he may want to do would be to strangle and kill a human being. Those who join the armed forces also might be in a similar situation: in a battle, a soldier is called upon to kill enemy soldiers, though he may not, outside his army life, kill a butterfly.

Thus, being ethical in a role and being ethical in personal life could mean quite different things. A remarkable demonstration of the extent to which people could be driven by the role expectations is provided by the famous experiments of Stanley Milgram (Box 10.1). Perfectly decent people resorted to inflicting (or so they thought) unbelievable cruelty on the subjects on the instructions of the experimenter, who told them that their role demanded it. You are probably familiar with the atrocities committed by the Nazis in the concentration camps, many of whom thought they were obeying orders, merely playing the role.

But there is always some dissonance when the values demanded by roles clash with personal value systems. Some learn to suppress their personal values; some can never really come to terms with what they have to do as part of the job and they may lose their sanity or attempt suicide. It is important to, therefore, clearly understand your value system, the demands from the role you are called upon to play, and their compatibility. In other words, you need to understand your moral sense.

BOX 10.1

Human Propensity for Obedience: The Milgram Experiments

These famous experiments on how far human beings will go just to be obedient were first conducted in 1961 by Stanley Milgram, a social psychologist from Yale University. The objective was to investigate the effects of authority and willingness for obedience. The experiments were meant to probe into the extent to which the atrocities conducted by Nazi prison guards on their prisoners

---

could be explained simply by their psychological need to obey orders from some authority.

In this experiment, there was a subject who played the role of a teacher, and a 'learner' who, unknown to the subject, was the researcher's collaborator. The 'teacher' and the 'learner' were in two separate rooms where they could communicate but not see each other. The teacher was to teach some word pairs to the learner, and test his response to questions. Whenever a question was wrongly answered, the teacher was to administer an electric shock to the learner as a punishment. There was actually no electric shock, but the 'teacher' did not know that; the 'learner' would cry out as if he was actually being subjected to an electric shock. The teacher thought he was administering the shock as he could hear the cries of the learner.

Progressively, the voltage at which the shocks were administered was increased. The 'learner' would act in a more and more desperate and pained tone, and tape-recorded sounds of the learner thumping on the door, begging the teacher to stop, etc. were played. The teacher would feel distressed and would want to stop the experiment, but the experimenter would urge him to continue in the interest of science. Even when the voltage reached 450 volts, more than enough to kill a person, most of the 'teachers' did not stop; they merely obeyed the experimenter, although they experienced great anguish. The experiment was terminated when the voltage reached 450 volts, and the 'teacher' was debriefed, told this was an experiment and the learner was an accomplice and had in fact not been subjected to any distress.

What percentage of people do you think actually go to this extent of causing pain and inflicting a possibly fatal punishment on the learner? Would you do it? When this question was posed to a group of people, less than 1 percent said that they would go to the extent of administering the highest level of punishment. But amazingly, about 65 percent of the subjects simply obeyed the experimenter and went all the way in administering the full shock. In some cases, the 'learner' pleaded that he had a heart condition but even so the 'teachers' continued, although they felt deeply distressed. The 'teachers' were perfectly normal, ordinary people, and were, by no stretch of imagination, sadists or psychologically disturbed people. The experiments were repeated with many types of people and in different countries and the results were broadly similar.

It would thus seem that being subjected to authority indeed makes people submissive and makes them do things they would not dream they would do. Their moral values can be subverted so easily.

If this was the result with an experimenter and some subjects over whom he had no real power, you can imagine what happens when bosses wield huge real power.

For an enactment of this experiment, see the ten-minute video at www.youtube.com/watch?v=y6GxluljT3w.

DEVELOPMENT OF A MORAL SENSE

Are human beings born with a moral sense? Is a moral sense inherent in human beings, or is it developed by the circumstances, by the environment in which they are brought up?

While there is no doubt that the environment such as the way you are parented, the children you play with in your childhood, the school you attend, etc. do play a role in shaping your values as you grow up, there is a great deal of evidence that children have an *inherent* sense of fairness, justice, and ethics. Thus when a small group of children are given cookies or pancakes to share, they tend to share them equally. Some interesting studies on this inherent moral sense are given in Box 10.2.

BOX 10.2

Development of Moral Sense

Do human beings have an inherent moral sense, a sense of fairness, or is it acquired? The economist James Harbaugh and his colleagues conducted a series of experiments, one of which was the so-called dictator game. In this game, there are two participants, A and B. A has, say, a bundle of $1 notes, amounting to $10 (the experiment has been conducted with different amounts of money to be shared) and A can give whatever he wants to B, who has to accept whatever is offered. The game is finished; it is a one-shot game, and this is made clear at the beginning itself. You would expect that since there is no next round and no consequences (this is announced in advance), *no one* would offer anything to the other person. Yet, when the game was played with many types of participants from different countries, races, income levels, and strangers versus known people (for example, students in the same class), while many offered nothing (as expected), a significant number (around 50 percent) offered to share the amount equally with B.

In a small variation (called the ultimatum game), while A could offer any amount to B, B has the option of taking that amount, in which case A keeps the balance, or refuses it, in which case both get nothing. Here two things happened. The number of people who offered nothing reduced (more people offered something) and interestingly, many who were offered $2 or less refused to take it. Rationally they should not do this because by their refusal, they stand to lose even the amount offered. Here, the motive was more like hurting A for his unfairness, even if that meant that B hurt himself in the process. There was thus more satisfaction in hurting A by depriving him of the larger share, than the cost of hurting himself by losing the smaller share offered. There was a perceived moral outrage.

These two experiments indicate a built-in sense of fairness in humans, as opposed to a purely rational approach to maximize gains. In the dictatorship situation, people shared something, in fact nearly half, as it was *fair to do so* (even though they were worse off as a result). In the ultimatum game, they tended to feel hurt and retaliated when treated unfairly.

These two experiments have been repeated among young school going children (aged five–seven). Surprisingly, the same pattern was repeated, although children younger than five tended to be more selfish. Thus not only is there an inherent sense of fairness, but it develops quite early in life. It seems that it is *not* natural to be selfish and appropriate as much as you can. This means that when you are forced to be unfair, a dissonance is set up; you feel uncomfortable.

As children grow older they develop other values as well, and among these is competitiveness. But there is still a sense of fair and unfair competition, which is best shown in the way children play games. It is only later that they discover the joys of cheating and gradually grow comfortable with it. When they are young, they do not consciously play any roles; they are just themselves. But soon, while playing, while in school, etc., they start understanding the meaning of roles, of how they should act not as they would like but as demanded by the role. Thus even in junior classes, students appointed as monitors become conscious of their power and use threats and punishment against other students. Later on, they could assume other roles such as representatives, student leaders, etc., and they learn to adapt their behaviour to their roles.

But it is when they enter organizations that they truly understand the demands of a role. In many cases they find that they are to obey certain rules and orders from above. It is then that they start experiencing true role conflicts. How they handle these conflicts is vital for their further development, not only as they climb up the hierarchy but as they develop as persons with a certain personality and character. Most people do not develop a stable value system and character for quite some time in their lives; their values do not get fully defined till quite late, and they do not learn to reconcile the conflicts satisfactorily.

Over a period of time, they learn to reconcile through a process similar to the learning process of experiencing, reflection, questioning of existing beliefs, and freezing a new set of beliefs. This is similar to the well-known 'learning-cycle model', given in Figure 10.1.

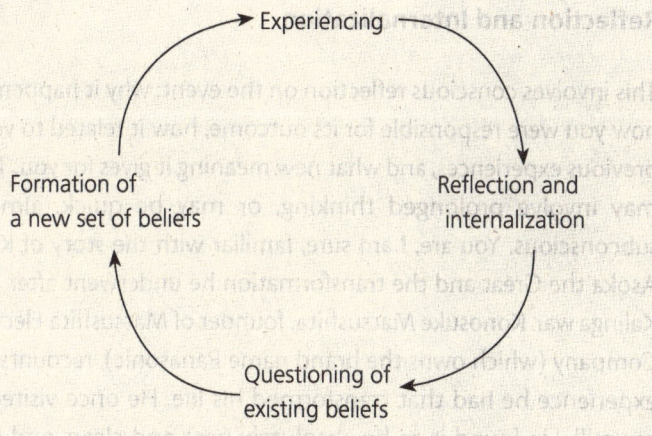

Figure 10.1: Values Development Cycle

Values Development Cycle

The cycle may be conceptualized as taking place in four stages, as may be seen from the diagram 10.1: experiencing, reflection and internalization, questioning of existing beliefs, and formation of a new set of beliefs. These are briefly explained below.

Experiencing

Experience is different from a mere happening. In a happening, events pass by without making any impression on the person, much like the objects seen from a moving train. The recipient is totally passive. But when the recipient becomes *active*, *interprets* the events, and *relates* them to his own previous experiences, faith and beliefs, and value system, they become experiences. Experiences thus create *meaning* for the recipient. Because of this, many experiences stick in your mind and are amenable for recall and reinterpretation.

Reflection and Internalization

This involves conscious reflection on the event: why it happened, how you were responsible for its outcome, how it related to your previous experiences, and what new meaning it gives for you. This may involve prolonged thinking, or may be quick, almost subconscious. You are, I am sure, familiar with the story of King Asoka the Great and the transformation he underwent after the Kalinga war. Konosuke Matsushita, founder of Matsushita Electric Company (which owns the brand name Panasonic), recounts an experience he had that transformed his life. He once visited a sawmill. He found it to be absolutely neat and clean, and the workers fully dedicated to their job. What impressed him the most was that the workers appeared to be so content and happy. The sawmill was actually a part of a Zen Buddhist temple, and Matsushita met the head of the temple to understand why this mill was so different. He was told that it was because the workers were not working for wages but for a larger purpose. Matsushita meditated there for some time and he saw things in a new light. He says that from that point onwards he did not see his enterprise as a mere commercial enterprise, but as a means to serve society, a notion he integrated into his 'Matsushita Philosophy' (Kotter, 1997).

What Matsushita did was to transform an event into an experience through a process of reflection. But he did not stop there; he went on to question his existing beliefs as well, which is Stage 3 in the cycle.

Questioning Existing Beliefs

Beliefs are formed over a period of time, and are reinforced through selective experiences. Once they are formed, they are difficult to modify, and this is especially so since the person gathers more 'evidence' in support of his beliefs, and rejects such information that does not support them. Thus a person who believes, say, that Muslims are violence prone and Hindus have suffered over centuries due to their weak and accommodating nature, keeps note of every riot and the number of Hindus killed, but conveniently does not look at the number of Muslims killed. Every act of terrorism by some Muslim is used as evidence to bolster his belief, and acts of terrorism or violence by Hindus is seen as rightful retaliation. The same can happen, of course, to a Muslim as well, Osama bin Laden being a prime example.

A good mind is not one which just clings to its beliefs, but one which can question them. Reflection involves keeping an open mind. Matsushita kept an open mind and got new insights. Buddha, after he walked out of his palace, joined a group of ascetics (called samanas) who practised extreme austerities and inflicted bodily pain on themselves, believing this was the way to find Truth. He realized, after some time, that this was not the way and proceeded to discover his own way. His earlier ideas were valid only till the next idea came and challenged them.

Managers are very prone to rigid belief systems. They develop stereotypes (as of course everyone does) of people, some notions on 'what works and what does not', and the best way to do things. These are simplifying mechanisms in the mind to cope with a hugely complex world. But they make them blind to reality and to the ethics of what they are doing. For example, a manager who believes that Keralites are prone to indiscipline and to strikes at the smallest pretext will exaggerate even a minor error by a Keralite employee, without giving him a second chance. Even today, certain castes and tribes are considered crime prone and are unfairly dealt with.

Modification of Existing Beliefs

Sometimes, not always, the new evidence and facts that have come to light may lead to the refining or revising of existing beliefs. Obviously, beliefs and values are not to be revised continuously, but there may be occasions when they need to be revised. More often, existing beliefs and values are refined. These crystallize into a stable value system, and the person is said to have developed his own character. Just as in plays and novels well-developed characters have a high degree of predictability about them and reveal who they are, people with character develop a degree of predictability about them. Being an ethical manager implies the development of such character.

The cycle continues—further experiences modify beliefs further. But after a time, sharp changes in values and character are unlikely.

What Should You, as an Ethical Manager, Do?

You need to actively understand and interpret the experiences you go through. Take time to reflect on their significance and understand what they mean to you. What did this experience tell you about yourself and your values? Do you know them better? Do your beliefs and values need any change?

Gandhi is the best example of a person who employed this principle in his life. He formed his basic values in his childhood from seeing plays based on the *Ramayana*, Sravana, and Harishchandra: the values of truth, service to others, and keeping one's word. He constantly read about different ways of looking at the world, notably Leo Tolstoy's work, which inspired him. His different experiences always led to reflection with the objective of becoming a better person. No wonder he named his autobiography *My Experiments with Truth*. For him, his whole life was an experiment. It was always to discover what life is all about, to understand what action produces what result.

An excellent example of this approach by Gandhi is how he reacted to the violence in South Africa (see Box 10.3).

> **BOX 10.3**
>
> Gandhi's Experiences with Apartheid in South Africa
>
> Mahatma Gandhi, then merely M.K. Gandhi, landed in South Africa in April 1893 to argue a case for an Indian businessman

settled there. Shortly after reaching Durban, he needed to go to Pretoria to meet his client. He purchased a first-class ticket and boarded the train.

When the train reached Pieter-Martizberg station in the middle of the night, a white man came into the compartment and called the train conductor to 'throw this coolie out of first class'. There were no laws preventing a non-white from travelling in first class, and Gandhi refused to get down and travel in the luggage van, as ordered by the ticket conductor. He, along with his belongings, was thrown out of the train onto the platform and the train left.

Gandhi shivered in the night in the waiting room (his overcoat was in his luggage which was taken by the Railway authorities) and then

I began to think of my duty. Should I fight for my rights or go back to India, or should I go to Pretoria without minding the insults, and return to India after finishing my case? It would be cowardice to run back to India without fulfilling my obligation. The hardship to which I was subjected was superficial—only a symptom of the deep disease of colour prejudice. I should try, if possible, to root out the disease and suffer hardships in the process. Redressal for wrongs I should seek only to the extent that would be necessary for the removal of the colour prejudice (Gandhi, 1927: 94).

Gandhi, in fact, spent the night on the platform reading the Holy Quran (which his friend had given him at the commencement of the journey) and tried to relate his experience with its teachings. It was thus a truly purposeful reflection and Gandhi understood how to relate the concepts of forgiveness and standing up for the weak to his life and he found a mission.

There were many such incidents in South Africa, such as his being beaten up by white goons and being thrown on a sidewalk by a white guard. In each case he refused to retaliate against his attackers, forgave them, and reinforced his belief that retaliation achieves nothing; objectives are better achieved through truth and non-violence. From these ideas emerged the idea of satyagraha, which he used to great effect in South Africa and, later, in India.

DOES PERCEIVED FAIRNESS DEPEND ON THE INTENTIONS?

Are actions judged purely on their own merit, or do the intentions behind an action affect the judgement of the action and its fairness? If the latter is true, then it is important to convey not only a decision or an action, but the intentions behind the action. It would seem that it is indeed important to make clear the intentions, and in such a way that the recipient audience believes in the stated intentions. Thus the ethics of an action is related to the way it is presented (see Box 10.4).

BOX 10.4

Fairness, Justice, and Intentions

You know that when courts give judgement in criminal cases a factor taken into account is the motive for the crime. In other words, an action is judged not only by the consequences, but also the motive behind it.

Surprisingly, even very young children seem to take into account the intent when they judge an event. Thus studies carried out with four-to-five-year-olds reveal that they can distinguish between a child turning on a hose to help her mother in watering the plants, and to dissolve her younger brother's sand castle; between a

---

chimpanzee leaping from a tree to injure another as against accidentally falling from a tree resulting in injuring another; and other similar situations. This was proved through a number of experiments conducted on children, through showing them clips of films that showed such different situations. The differences in context were not obvious because the children had to make out the context and the intention purely from the film, with no explanations.

Even simple changes in words can alter the perceived intentions and the judgement. Consider the following scenario, outlined by Marc Hauser (2006: 51):

> The Vice President of a company goes to the CEO and says, 'We are thinking of starting a new programme. It will help us increase profits, and it will also harm the environment.' The CEO answers, 'I don't care at all about the environment. I just want to make as much profit as I can. Let us start the programme.' They start the programme. Sure enough, it causes damage to the environment, as anticipated.
>
> When asked how much blame the CEO deserves for what he did, the overwhelming majority of respondents tend to say that the CEO deserves the full blame.
>
> But if the word 'help' replaces the word 'harm' in the statement, 'improves' replaces 'causes damage' and 'praise' replaces 'blame', the responses tend to be that the CEO deserves little praise for helping the environment. While in the former case the harm is intentional, in the latter case, the help is unintentional.

ON BECOMING AN ETHICAL MANAGER

The first step towards becoming an ethical manager is the same as for becoming a leader: knowing yourself and discovering your true values. For, leadership has ethics as a vital component. A leader is one who leads people not in *some* direction but in the *right* direction. That is why people like Hitler and Stalin fail the true test of leadership: they led people all right, but was it in the right direction? For discovering what the right direction is, you need to know yourself. How well do you know yourself? This may seem to be a trivial question, but actually a good degree of self-awareness is the exception rather than the rule. What are your core strengths and weaknesses? What are the situations when you are comfortable, and when you are highly uncomfortable? How strong are your convictions, and to what extent are you prepared to stand up for them?

To arrive at an answer to these questions, you need to engage yourself in a process of introspection. It is amazing that people give time to so many people but none to themselves. You need to take some time to be yourself, to reflect on the events of the day and on their significance.

The question invariably turns to what you want from life. This reflects your values. It is only well after you pass your teens that your values become clear. When you are young, everything seems attractive and desirable and you find it difficult to make consistent choices, whatever they are. As you mature, you get progressively more comfortable with some situations and less so with others, and develop the courage to reject some seemingly attractive alternatives; you learn to take a stand. Gradually other people get a better idea of what they can expect of you, which is the starting point of the development of your character.

When a person joins an organization, a conflict in values begins. There are some clear rules in an organization, but most of what is important is unwritten, and is picked up near the water cooler or during coffee breaks: 'This is the way things are done here', and 'This is how you go up here'. These develop into a pattern of behaviour, at first in the organization, and later, perhaps it pervades your personal life as well. Not all of these learnings have ethical implications, but many have indirect implications.

For example, whenever an accident occurs in the Railways, an 'interdepartmental' enquiry committee is formed to unravel the cause of the accident. This is the *stated objective*, but each functional department officer is expected not to find the real cause of the accident, but to 'support' his department, that is, to ensure that the responsibility is not fixed on his department. When responsibility gets fixed on one department, this leads to considerable pressure on the concerned officer to 'better examine' the evidence; tampering of evidence is not unknown. The officer concerned is forced to adopt what he knows are unethical and unprofessional practices.

Organizations routinely set objectives that are virtually unattainable and would need shortcuts. The management, while professing to be ethical, may turn a blind eye to such shortcuts and ultimately lose control over who does what. People find it impossible to be ethical and to continue in such organizations. They have to adapt; if they cannot, they have no alternative but to quit. Often, this becomes a harsh choice. But in the long run, if there is a great disconnect between your basic values and the demands from the organization, it would be better for you to quit at an opportune time and find another organization where you are a better fit.

To be able to get into such a state of mind, you need to develop a perspective. It is hard to define what perspective is, but it is quite easy to tell who does not have it. It is the ability to see and understand many issues and their implications all together, integrate them, and get a holistic picture. This comes through experience and conscious broadening of your mind. Reading widely can give you glimpses of the dilemmas of life and discussion with others on substantive issues is a known way of broadening your mind. Today, the internet helps in locating excellent sources to get multiple points of view; you could also get on to blogs and discussion forums. What you do with your time outside work may be more important than what you do during work.

But in today's hyper-competitive world, how does one find the spare time? This is an important question, but often it is really a question of what you do with the time you have. An extraordinary amount of time is wasted in parties, get-togethers, and gossip sessions even during work. It is amazing what you would find if you take an inventory of what you do with your time by keeping a diary and looking at it after a week.

Warren Bennis, the great leadership thinker, has noted that the best leaders always find time to read a variety of books and magazines. They work very hard, put in long hours at office but still find time to read in a variety of ways: during flights, on weekends and holidays, while waiting for a meeting, and so on. It really comes down to not how much time you have, but to what you do with the time you have.

ANATOMY OF FALL FROM GRACE

On May 18, 2011, *Mint* carried an article on one of India's greatest achievers. He had established for himself a stellar reputation, rose to head one of the most respected firms in the world, was involved in a number of philanthropic activities, and did a lot for India. Today, he is under a cloud for some serious misdemeanours, and has had to step down from the membership of boards of some prestigious companies. Such charges were unthinkable about him, say, five years ago.

In May 2011, the Chief of the International Monetary Fund (IMF) was accused of attempting to rape a hotel maid and was put in prison; he had to step down from his position in the IMF, and his dreams of becoming the President of France lay in tatters.

Another big name in India's corporate circle, who built one of India's most successful IT companies, Satyam (ironically, the word *satyam* means 'truth' in Sanskrit and in many Indian languages), was involved in a number of philanthropic activities, and was responsible for setting up the 108 accident service, is in jail from January 2009 and in his case, he has confessed to one of the largest frauds in Indian corporate history till date (see Box 10.5).

BOX 10.5

The Scandalous Satyam

In 2008, Satyam was India's fourth largest IT company, with clients around the world. Its founder and CEO, Ramalinga Raju, was well known and respected, and had earned awards such as the Ernst & Young Entrepreneur of the Year in 2008, and the Golden Peacock Award for Corporate Governance and Compliance in 2008.

On December 17, 2008, Raju announced plans to acquire two companies, Maytas Infra and Maytas Properties, both owned by members of his family. The rationale was to diversify Satyam's business portfolio to avoid being tied to the IT services market. However, the stockholders strongly protested these acquisitions. They believed that only Raju and his family would benefit from the acquisition but Satyam would not.

In December 2008, the stock price of Satyam started declining due to some news items about difficulties it was having with the World Bank on ethical issues. Though the company denied it, three major outside directors resigned from Satyam's board of directors. The company was coming to a position where it was seriously running out of cash, although its books showed a

---

comfortable position. On January 7, 2009, Raju sent a letter to the Satyam board of directors and India's Securities and Exchange Commission, admitting his involvement in overstating the amount of cash held by Satyam in its balance sheet by about $1 billion. Furthermore, Satyam had a liability for $253 million arranged for his personal use, and he had overstated Satyam's September 2008 quarterly revenues by 76 percent and its quarterly profits by 97 percent. This announcement sent shockwaves through corporate India and through India's stock market. Not only did Satyam's stock price suffer greatly (78 percent decline) but the overall market decreased by 7.3 percent on the day of the announcement.

Sadly, Satyam stood now for anything but the truth. Raju was arrested and charged, and the shareholders lost a great deal of their wealth. The company was taken over by Tech Mahindra and has been salvaged partially, but there is no doubt that corporate governance in India has taken a big hit and its reputation has been tarnished.

Such tales of fall from grace of highly respected people, who were greatly successful and had no need to indulge in the kind of activities they had or alleged to have indulged in, raises a question: What happened? Why did they do it? Can something happen to otherwise perfectly normal and respected people that suddenly makes their ethical orientation go haywire? Are there any pitfalls that you need to avoid?

I identify four such pitfalls we would all like to avoid: (a) the corrupting influence of power leading to (b) a sense of invincibility; (c) ambition without purpose; and (d) suppression of guilt through rationalization, so that you stop believing you are doing anything wrong at all.

Corrupting Influence of Power

Lord Acton's dictum that power corrupts, and absolute power corrupts absolutely seems to work in a large number of cases. As they ascend in hierarchy, people whose ethical standards are under no question gain in power. If they are successful, they start believing in the infallibility of themselves. They take greater and greater risks with their ethical positions, as, for example, in succumbing to bribery, doing a private business on the side, and insider trading. Many executives, when they become senior, stop listening to anybody and understanding the implications of their action. Bala Balachandran, the highly respected professor in Kellogg Business School and the founder of the Great Lakes Institute of Management, Chennai, said in an interview about such a person who fell from grace and to whom he had said:

> You are an eagle, so why do you want to be with these chicken who can't fly? You will get the chicken flu.

Feeling of Invincibility and Infallibility

This state of mind, of being supremely self-confident, unwilling to listen to other points of view, and confident of handling any situation that may arise, is best described by the Greek word 'hubris'. This is the pride that goeth, as the saying goes, before a fall. And the fall, when it comes, is steep and heavy, and as happened in the case of Bernard Madoff, who ran a notorious ponzi scheme through his firm Bernard L. Madoff Investment Securities LLC, can lead to humiliating incarceration in jail, and tragically, his son, Mark Madoff, unable to face the ignominy, committed suicide.

Ambition without Purpose

Leaders and successful managers are usually people with a lot of ambition. They seem to be dissatisfied with the status quo and wish to improve it, with themselves being the agents for improvement. An important component of this ambition is *purpose*: a larger purpose towards which the ambition is directed. This purpose needs to extend beyond yourself; it needs to have a superordinate goal that sets out how it will impact others in the organization, community, and society. This way there is a constant touchstone against which you could test your action: Is it only to further your interests or does it address larger issues?

Ayn Rand will perhaps not agree to such an approach: unabashed personal pursuit of selfish and individualistic interest, she will argue, is the purpose of life. But when this happens, it becomes a wild pursuit of further personal aggrandizement (as distinct from achievement): a person having hundreds of millions of dollars aspires to become a billionaire and indulges in unethical activities.

There are some people who state their goals in terms of what they want to *have*, as compared to what they want to *be*. This is ambition, but without purpose. Wanting to be a billionaire is an ambition, but it cannot be a purpose.

Guilt Suppression through Rationalization

Rationalization is a well-known psychological mechanism to suppress guilt and continue to do what you know is wrong. While reasoning proceeds from arguments to a conclusion, rationalization is just the opposite: it starts from a conclusion and finds arguments to justify it. For example, bribe-taking may be rationalized by such arguments as 'everyone does it', 'the bribe is small', 'the person giving it to me can afford it', and so on. If you are sure that you are going to do a certain thing, arguments are not difficult to come by. Such rationalization is invariably built on flimsy arguments that erode the ethical base of the person.

The factors above affect a person's judgement. Like in a poker game winning can lead to irrational bets being placed, you may realize it is too late if you are unwilling to look honestly at the implications of your actions.

Rationalization has a tendency to escalate. Many people proceed on the slippery path of ethical transgression, committing a greater transgression at each step. Initially it is a minor gratification, then a greater one, and so on and each stage is rationalized to suppress the sense of guilt. This behaviour extends all the way from corruption scandals to insider trading, fraud, and crimes against humanity.

What Should You, an Ethical Manager, Do?

You need to be aware of the pitfalls outlined above. You can ask yourself questions such as:

1. Do I dare take an outside opinion? Am I courageous enough to hear that opinion and face up to what that implies?

2. How readily do my subordinates agree to my positions? Do they agree all too readily?

3. Is my ambition only for myself? Does it have a larger purpose?

4. Am I honestly making reasoned arguments and reaching a conclusion or rationalizing a pre-reached conclusion?

CONCLUSION

Becoming an ethical manager is essentially a personal process of development. This starts with the process of understanding yourself, what your true core beliefs and values are, and what you really want to achieve in life. This involves reflection and crystallization of your values further and further as one matures. This takes place very differently in life for different persons; in fact, in some persons it does not take place at all, and in some cases, it even takes a negative turn. A good way to understand this process is to read M.K. Gandhi's autobiography, *My Experiments with Truth* (1927), and to see the excellent movie, *The Making of the Mahatma* (1996) by Shyam Benegal.

To what extent you want to become an ethical manager, or even whether to become one at all, is a personal decision. It cannot be pursued through a consequentialist approach (as applied to yourself): you pursue ethics not because it is *more profitable* (though it may indeed be so) but it is *simply the right thing to do*. The same is true about the path taken to reach there. There are several ways, and you need to take the path you are more comfortable with. Failure to understand your value system often leads to fall from grace and, often, ignominy.

The fall from grace often happens slowly and without your even realizing it. Each step is advanced one tiny step at a time, and it cumulates into a colossal mistake without your being conscious of it. This is an insidious process and often you realize it only when a rude jolt leads to the fall from grace. Then it is a complete change in life unlike a slip due to lack of competency, for, while competence slip-ups or errors in judgement can be redeemed, ethical slip-ups do not restore the status quo ante. The person is no longer the same.

Thus the challenge is to not only become an ethical manager, but to stay one.

KEY TAKEAWAYS

1. Besides acquired values, human beings have an innate moral sense. This needs to be nurtured.

2. As a child grows older, he learns to reconcile different values and ethical imperatives. He develops his own unique ethical personality.

3. The process is akin to the well-known learning cycle, namely, experience, reflection, re-examination of old values and formation of new ones.

4. Through this process, a person should come to know himself. A good leader or an ethical manager knows who he is.

5. The fall from grace is easy, and the root causes can be traced to power and its corroding influence, development of hubris and a sense of invincibility and infallibility, soaring ambition without a larger purpose, and guilt suppression through rationalization. Managers would do well to pause and think on whether they are affected by these factors.

REFERENCES

Benegal, S. (dir.). 1996. *The Making of the Mahatma.*

Gandhi, M.K. 1927. *An Autobiography or the Story of My Experiments with Truth.* Ahmedabad: Navjeevan Trust.

Kotter, J. 1997. *Matsushita Leadership.* New York: Free Press.

Hauser, M. 2006. *Moral Minds: How Nature Designed Our Universal Sense of Right and Wrong.* New York: HarperCollins.

11

Ethics and Management Education

'I never let my schooling interfere with my learning.'

—Mark Twain

Recent scandals involving companies such as Enron, Worldcom, and Satyam have focused attention on the role of management education in creating a better ethical climate in the world of business. Many critics seem to go overboard in blaming management schools for the state of affairs, as if it is the schools that have created an attitude of indifference to ethics in the minds of managers. Of course, nineteenth-century America was notorious for the huge frauds and cheating that took place in many of its industries, notably railroads, much before the advent of the MBA programme. Nor was the UK in the eighteenth and nineteenth centuries an example of probity in business dealings. Yet it is widely felt that management schools have contributed in some way to the 'scandal economies' of today. (In India, fortunately, management schools are not blamed, at least not much; perhaps our scamsters get along very well without an MBA!) The feeling that management education has indeed played a role in the deterioration of ethical standards, and definitely *should* play a more active role in improving it, seems to be widespread, and management educators need to question themselves as to whether they could play a more proactive role in this field than they have been doing so far.

In this chapter, I do not propose to evaluate the contribution, if any, of management schools to the seemingly deteriorating ethical climate in business, nor am I interested in either accusing or defending management schools regarding their role concerning ethics in business. What I seek to do is simply explore ways in which they *could* play a constructive role in improving the ethical climate.

MANAGEMENT EDUCATION: A MISNOMER?

There is a distinction between vocational training and education. Vocational training seeks to impart specific skills required for a job. This need not refer to manual labour; a pilot's training is vocational training, and so is a chartered accounts' course (CA in India). So is law; so is teachers' training.

Education, however, is different from vocational training and has a different objective. It does not seek to teach any specific skill as such; even if it does deal with imparting knowledge, this is not to do a specific job. Its objective is not to produce a person who is job ready or even employable. The true role of education is to broaden the minds of the students and to enable them to see and understand issues of life in a better perspective. Thus a good curriculum should contain not only the 'core' subjects but also topics on humanities and philosophy that can broaden students' minds.

Management education is a fairly recent development; it started mainly in the 1950s. As it was first conceived, management education concerned itself with the development of the needed skills for managing an enterprise. Thus, in some sense, it was vocational training. But from the beginning it was also widely recognized that pure skill inputs (such as accounting or drawing a flowchart) are not adequate, and management education needed to give broader inputs such as on behavioural and interpersonal skills. But many B-schools soon reduced these soft skills to those needed specifically in a manager's job rather than fitting them into a broader context. Further, 'soft' courses were generally not patronized by students the way 'hard-core' courses such as those on finance or strategy were, as may be seen from the pattern of electives students prefer to take in most MBA courses, no doubt because the latter are seen as bettering their potential to get good jobs.

No matter what is said in the induction lecture of a B-school to its new students at the beginning of a programme, students, when they come to their first classes, are told in no uncertain terms that managers of an enterprise are the agents of the shareholders and their prime duty is to maximize the profit on behalf of their shareholders. This is the basic framework around which all the courses are built.

In recent years, stung by (perhaps undeserved) criticism, B-schools have introduced mandatory courses on ethics, often in the first weeks of the programme. These are often well-drawn-up courses and interesting discussions could take place in the class, but their effect tends to last only till the end of the class. Any impact they might have had withers in the next class, probably on microeconomics focused on—you guessed it—profit maximization! Even worse, ethics is reduced to a set of skills and considered useful because it also contributes to maximization of profits in the long run.

Such a curriculum can hardly be said to qualify as true education for it fails to take students (or participants of management development programmes) to a higher mental and intellectual plane. The typical MBA programme does not even pretend to do that.

Some management schools have consciously tried to integrate ethics into their overall programme structure. For instance, courses on ethics based not on case studies and abstract readings but on literature have been introduced. I shall return to this theme later, but such schools remain few.

ETHICS AS AN INTEGRAL PART OF MANAGEMENT SCHOOL CURRICULUM

Even though it may be argued that values are well formed in a person's personality by the time he comes to the MBA (in which case why blame B-schools?), the reality is that values keep changing throughout his life, based on new inputs and experiences. And few would doubt that for most students the MBA is indeed a new experience which leaves a lasting impression on the minds of students. Hence B-schools could create a different kind of experience during the MBA by giving a holistic perspective on what business and business education is all about.

This involves teaching not ethics as such, but ethical aspects of running a business, as a part of the overall management of a business, with the different stakeholders. That is why, in this book, I have organized ethical issues around the interfaces of the firm with its different stakeholders and those who interact with it. During the different courses that are concerned predominantly with one stakeholder, as, for example, marketing with customers, HR with employees, and strategy with environment, the instructors should strive to look at the ethical aspects of the decisions students are trained to take, not just the logical and analytical solutions proposed by them. The objective of such teaching should be not to evaluate a decision as ethical or unethical, but to understand the nuances and the tradeoffs involved and help students to learn to strike a balance. For example, in a marketing class, how do students get to weigh the additional profits brought in by overpricing versus the overt reactions that it could produce in the minds of its consumers? Should the firm care about them? Or when discussing a remarkably creative advertisement that is likely to catch the attention of consumers (and possibly increase sales), the instructors can discuss the ethical aspects of this advertisement as well. Or in a class on HR, the ethical aspects of target setting, performance appraisal, and compensation could also be discussed.

This points to the different roles B-schools can play in not only teaching business ethics as such, but also in developing a more holistic picture of managing an enterprise. If the objective of B-schools is to bring as much reality as possible into the classroom, then it is also to be recognized that ethics is a part of reality. Business decisions—at least the major ones—are rarely taken in a reductionist analytical manner, that is, by taking a problem apart and solving each part separately; in real life, they are treated holistically and managers' values do enter these decisions. Thus by integrating ethics into every subject (rather than as a standalone topic), it would be possible to bring about a higher degree of richness in management education. B-schools will turn out better (not merely more analytical) managers. Students can be asked to take an overall stand on every issue and to reflect on the underlying value system that led them to take such a stand.

TOWARDS A BROADER CURRICULUM

Managing, especially at higher levels, is not about being more analytical but about having a better perspective, about understanding human nature and developing the ability to hold multiple, often contradictory, ideas simultaneously in your mind (I am excluding certain jobs such as consulting, equity analysis, investment banking, etc., which are essentially based on individual knowledge and skills and are not really managerial at all). These cannot be achieved through developing a rationalistic, analytical mode of thinking alone. They have to be achieved by encouraging managers to think in a different way, to become more comfortable with dealing with unstructured problems, and developing the ability to see multiple points of view. These are not necessarily included in a typical B-school curriculum. That is why B-schools tend to churn out MBAs, not managers, as the noted management thinker Henry Mintzberg has observed in his book *Managers, not MBAs: } A Hard Look at the Soft Practice of Managing and Management Development* (2004). Srikant M. Datar, David G. Garvin, and Patrick G. Cullen of Harvard Business School, in their recent book *Rethinking the MBA: Business Education at a Crossroads* (2010), argue for a different curriculum that, among other things, helps students develop leadership skills along with knowledge about management.

There is a need to broad base the management education curriculum to include liberal arts such as philosophy, history, literature, and the fine arts, and to make management education move from its vocational training mode to a true education mode. Such courses are now increasingly being adopted in some top B-schools. For example, Harvard Business School runs a course on ethics and leadership (by Joseph Badaracco) through literature. MIT's Sloan School has a course where students have to enact Shakespeare's *Henry V*. Wharton has a compulsory MBA workshop titled 'Leadership through the Arts' facilitated by the world-renowned dance company Pilobolus, in which students explore movement, improvisation, and collaborative choreography. IIMA has courses on leadership and ethics based on literature, run by Asha Kaul and me. Films are an excellent vehicle for teaching ethics as, for example, the movies *Wall Street* (1987), *Lord of the Flies*

(1963), and *To Kill a Mocking Bird* (1962). It is during the experience of those teaching these courses (and the students who take these courses) that invaluable insights are generated in discussions and the participants find themselves enriched.

HOW DO B-SCHOOLS FACE THEIR OWN ETHICAL DILEMMAS?

B-schools, like the enterprises discussed earlier, also have to face their own dilemmas. How they resolve them gives a clue as to what extent they put in practice their own teachings.

For example, how do they deal with students' copying and downloading answers from the internet without acknowledgement (this has become a huge problem in all B-schools)? If students are found to have copied in their submissions or found copying during examinations, how does the B-school deal with it? Is a lenient attitude to the offending students really fair to the students who have worked hard? Students and the public generally come to know of how a B-school tackles these problems and how serious they are of their ethical professions. Their credibility and stature depend not only on what they teach, but also on what they do.

When it comes to teachers, the problem attains a different dimension. How serious is the B-school in dealing with ethical problems with teachers, such as plagiarism? If a star professor is found to have indulged in plagiarism, how does the school deal with it? (This is similar to the Type-4 manager encountered earlier in this book.) How does the B-school deal with this person? There could be other ethical transgressions such as indifferent or unfair grading, seeking sexual favours (especially from doctoral students), and so on. How does the B-school deal with such complaints?

B-schools necessarily have to observe high ethical standards and set an example. To what extent a school earns a reputation for doing this will affect its credibility.

B-SCHOOLS DO HAVE A RESPONSIBILITY

I believe B-schools are not responsible for all that a person does after graduation in his subsequent career, whether good or bad. It is silly to think that what a person has become in the first twenty or twenty-five years of life can be corrected and undone during a one- or two-year stay at a B-school. Similarly, what a person does twenty years after graduation, after being exposed to a variety of situations, opportunities, frustrations, and temptations, can hardly be attributed to the B-school stay which was supposed to have taught him the role of profit maximization. If your bonus is tied to profit, it requires no B-schooling to see that maximization of profits is indeed profitable to yourself.

But my argument is that B-schools do have a responsibility all the same. First, they face ethical dilemmas just as industry managers do. How they face and resolve them serves as a message to the outside world. Whatever one may say, education can never be just a commercial transaction; it is about being a role model. We expect from our teachers, often unrealistically, a standard of behaviour that is exemplary. Hence B-schools have the responsibility to show as action what they preach.

Second, B-schools have a responsibility to bring ethics as a part of the curriculum. Ethics need not be taught as a separate subject; it can be woven into all the other subjects, but this needs to be done. There could be conscious efforts to direct a student's way of thinking oriented solely to profit maximization, or into thinking that ethics have no place in business decisions.

Third, newer methodologies and design of curriculum could be devised consciously to enable students to think for themselves about their values, the way they see and react to ethical dilemmas, and compare it to how others see it. The value of management education lies not only in what a student learns from a teacher, but also in what he learns from peers and from his own reflection. Unfortunately, the B-school curriculum is so fast paced that there is really no time for reflection and growth.

It is my experience that MBA students, especially in India (where they come without too much work experience), do want to think, grow, and (this may come as a surprise to many of the readers) develop their moral sense. B-schools have been teaching that a firm is essentially an economic entity. It is time to teach that they are more than that.

SO WHAT SHOULD A B-SCHOOL TEACHER AND ADMINISTRATOR DO?

1. The B-school top management (directors/deans, heads) must be clear as to whether they are in the business of mere management skills training or in management education. There needs to be more of an education element in it.

2. You need to ask: What is the stance of my B-school regarding business ethics? Is it a lip service or is it taken seriously?

3. You need to ask: Is ethics taught to all? If so, how? Pulpit preaching takes you nowhere. Business ethics is more about resolution of dilemmas than about understanding absolute moral dos and don'ts. Ethics need to be woven into every subject and students need to be encouraged to think about

the moral aspects of a decision as well as the economic aspects.

4. You could devise a broader curriculum that could approach ethical aspects innovatively, as, for example, literature, history, and playacting.

5. Ethics is not so much about knowing and learning as reflecting and being able to do what, *under the circumstances*, is the right thing to do. This requires time for reflection. You, as a management teacher, could encourage students and managers to ask: Am I giving enough time to myself for reflection? What does it lead to?

6. Last, you need to realize that two years in a B-school are only a small part of the life of a manager. All the good and bad things they do later on are not due to what they learnt in B-school. So there is no point in being apologetic beyond a point.

REFERENCES

Brook, P. (dir.). 1963. *Lord of the Flies*. (A feature film)

Datar, S. M., D. G. Garvin, and P. G. Cullen. 2010. *Rethinking the MBA: Business Education at a Crossroads*. Boston: Harvard Business School Press.

Ghoshal, S. 2005. 'Bad Management Theories are Destroying Good Management Practices'. *Academy of Management Learning and Education*, 4 (1), March.

Mintzberg, H. 2004. *Managers, not MBAs: A Hard Look at the Soft Practice of Managing and Management Development*. San Francisco: Berret-Koehler Publishers.

Mulligan, R. (dir.). 1962. *To Kill a Mockingbird*. (A feature film)

Stone, O. (dir.). 1987. *Wall Street*. (A feature film)

Conclusion: The Difficulty of Being Ethical

'The unexamined life is not worth living.'

—Socrates

I have tried to show in the earlier chapters that the problem in business ethics is often (not always) not one of choosing wrong versus right, but between two alternatives, both partly right, both partly wrong. It is not just a question of polluting or not polluting, but polluting at what cost and to what extent. There are, of course, some choices that are clearly unethical as, for example, accepting bribes or molesting a woman employee. There is no ethical dilemma involved here. But many business decisions do not present a clear right or wrong question, but are in the nature of dilemmas. Ethical dilemmas are those situations where it is difficult to see not what is right or wrong, good or bad, but which choice is *relatively better under the circumstances*. This is the difficulty of being good, being ethical.

The title of this chapter is taken from the title of a recent book of the same name by Gurcharan Das. In this superb book, Das, who was the CEO of Procter & Gamble (P&G), India, and has held various positions in that organization in India and abroad, examines the ethical issues posed by the *Mahabharata* and how to resolve them.

Unlike the *Ramayana* which deals with ideal characters, the *Mahabharata* deals with real life, real characters, and real dilemmas. It is not a conflict between pure good and evil. Everyone has to confront ethical dilemmas and resolve them in their own way.

For example, Karna has to choose between his sworn loyalty to his friend Duryodhana and dharma, or righteousness. (Though the Pandavas were not lily-white, they were at least entitled to their kingdom after their thirteen years of exile as per the terms at the game of dice.) Bhishma has to make a similar choice between loyalty to the kingdom of Hastinapura and adharma. Yudhishtira has to choose between upholding the dignity of Draupadi and keeping his word at the game of dice (even though he was cheated). Even Krishna has to choose between breaking the rules of war (while getting Bhishma, Drona, Karna, and Duryodhana killed) and losing the war. Each of them *know* what the issues are, *know* that they are making deliberate choices and *have* to make them. Problems do not go away by closing your eyes to them; you do not know the consequences of the alternatives (who would have thought that the game of dice would lead to Draupadi's *vastraharan*?) and yet have to make choices. Yudhishtira wants to avert the war but as a king, he has also to carry out the duty his role demands, as pointed out by Kunti and Krishna. (For a discussion on what the *Mahabharata*'s characters can teach us about ethics, see S. Manikutty [forthcoming]).

As in the *Mahabharata*, ethical issues in business are complex and existentialist. The past has happened, wrongs cannot be undone, and you need to move forward. The future is entirely unknown. The present is the only time you have, and you have to decide here, and now. Not doing anything is an option that also has its own consequences. As a business manager you do not have the luxury Balarama had of staying neutral, without taking sides. Your role demands something, your relations and family demand something else, and your personal values tell you to do something else. You have to reconcile them. You need to make compromises, compromises that you don't like to make but have to make, at the same time making sure that the compromise does not become a sellout. It is a delicate balance to be found by every manager.

Indeed, such a balance needs to be found in many dimensions. For example, too much adherence to a point of view would be rigidity, while too little would be vacillation and unpredictability. Seeing only one point of view may be construed as tunnel vision, trying to accommodate all points of view may be seen as indecisiveness.

How do you strike a balance among these conflicting demands? For doing this, you need to develop *perspective*. This is the ability to see, understand, and appreciate many points of view, understand their relative importance, and arrive at *your own* point of view.

Developing such a perspective requires a broadening of the mind. Life has many facets and you have to see, experience, and assimilate them. Go back to the learning cycle outlined in Chapter 10: experience, reflection, and assimilation, questioning of existing belief systems, and forming new ones. It is a process of constant refinement and evolution.

To develop these, you need to learn to look at life in its myriad forms. Humanities, it is being increasingly realized, are a vital input in the making of leaders. Reading good literature, watching good plays and movies, and enlightened conversation help in developing better perspectives. Humanities offer an excellent way to understand life situations and dilemmas, get a handle on human behaviour, and be better equipped and prepared for facing dilemmas.

Facing such dilemmas involves preparation. Just as a pilot is trained to prepare for unlikely emergencies and kept trained through repeated simulations, a manager needs to train his mind to face such situations so that when they come, he knows what to do.

To return to what I said in Chapter 2, ethical theories help to give some insights into the structure of ethical problems but cannot tell you how to solve them. For, these theories, while trying to show what is ethical and what is not, skirt the real problem, which is how to choose among seemingly right or wrong alternatives. You may not be wiser on this even after reading all of Kant's works or, for that matter, Bentham's, Hume's, or Rawls'. They may give some points of view but the choice is to be made by you and only you.

DO ETHICS PAY?

This is an important question. Managers are there to show 'results' and their career depends on the results shown over years. Do ethics pay in this reality? If, as a result of ethical actions, a manager's performance goes down, is it worth it?

It first depends upon the meaning of the term 'pay'. The 'payoff' may be in many forms, and bonuses and promotions may be only one of them. In government service, officers constantly come across situations where an ethical stand may involve coming in conflict with a superior or a politician. Consider a 'professional' act like a postmortem by a doctor. Doctors are often pressurized to give a certain result to suit a particular interest. Police officers are constantly pressurized to arrest or not arrest someone, and conduct an investigation in a particular way or even deliberately botch it so that the accused will get acquitted for lack of evidence. Not going by these dictates from 'above' could mean considerable damage to your career. It does seem as if it does not 'pay' to stand up for what you believe is right.

Life does not necessarily reward the right or the good, even in the long run. In the famous film *Lord of the Flies* (based on the 1954 novel of the same name by William Golding), basic human nature is explored in a 'back-to-a-clean-state' situation. The film is an exploration of the conflict between a leader who tries to maintain his ethical position throughout and one who is thoroughly unscrupulous. It shows the progressive triumph of the unscrupulous and the ethical leader escapes getting killed at the end only by providence. It leaves you with disturbing questions (see Box 12.1).

BOX 12.1

Lord of the Flies

This novel by William Golding (1954) has become required reading in many schools and colleges in literature courses. The film starts with an airplane with a group of students crashing on an island and though all the children (below age thirteen) survive, they have no hope of being rescued. They now start organizing their lives as demanded by their new reality. There are two central characters, Ralph and Jack. Jack was earlier a choir leader and some of the boys belonged to his choir. The group elects Ralph as their leader. The children are scared and hungry, and need someone to give them hope, confidence, and food. Ralph, assisted by the brainy but non-charismatic Piggy, tries to chalk out an agenda for maximizing their chances of rescue through starting a fire, setting the rules of behaviour, and for hunting for food. Ralph is considerate to his group and is never harsh but tries to take his followers along. He never resorts to violence. He is, in fact, a perfect example of a textbook leader.

Jack, who wants to be the leader, undermines Ralph by forming a separate group, promising them meat. He claims to be a brave and fearless hunter. He entices more and more of the group members by a clever combination of temptation, threats, and often, brutal punishments to instil fear. He has no sense of values and is prepared to go to any extent to quell disobedience. He relies on emotions, the worst aspects of human nature and, despite (or because of) being completely unethical, becomes the leader of practically the whole crowd. He has no compunctions about killing Piggy and another student who follows Ralph, and torturing two students who do not submit to his authority.

The story ends with a frenzied chase to get hold of and kill Ralph and this is just about to happen when a helicopter lands and rescues the whole crowd.

The novel is written in such a way that as you progress through it, you may find yourself saying, 'Yes, this is how it happens in the real world'. It seems that power and ruthlessness are the main drivers. It does not provide a happy ending and a moral of the story that goodness ultimately triumphs. Even in the competitive business world, ruthless and unscrupulous competition leads to the draconian dictum of the survival of the fittest, not the 'good and ethical', then what is the justification for being ethical?

For an answer, turn back to the *Mahabharata*. The story definitely does not carry the message that truth and goodness triumph. While the Kauravas never suffer and enjoy all the good things in life, including the kingdom, for the Pandavas, barring a few years ruling in Indraprastha, life has been nothing but misery. Even the war gives them a hollow victory and Duryodhana, before dying, mockingly welcomes Yudhishtira to his newly won kingdom of widows and orphans. None of Draupadi's children survive to inherit the kingdom. Yudhishtira wonders whether it was worth it all, and poses the question to Krishna.

Krishna's answer is that it was all worth it, not for just the end result but for the process of education it has put him through. He has to be a dharmic king because the concept needs to be established. That is more important than whether ultimately Yudhishtira was better off or otherwise in his long journey of education.

Here lies the starkness of the question: If you are to be ethical only because it pays, this overlooks one of the elements of being human. Only human beings can make *ethical* choices. This is the message conveyed by Don Quixote in Cervantes' immortal novel as well.

You can turn around the question and ask: Does being unethical necessarily pay? For every person who has made it good through unethical means, there is also one who has suffered. And for every person who has been ethical and has suffered, there is also one who has succeeded by establishing his credentials as a person of integrity. Life does not promise you anything for being ethical, but it does not promise you anything for being unethical either.

It all ultimately comes to personal choices, choices regarding what you want to *be* rather than what you want to *do*. You need to ask yourself whether you wish to lead a glamorous, 'successful' life or a perhaps monotonous life, or a life with passion as well as compassion, to be well regarded, and someone for whom many will cry when you die.

Socrates once said, 'The unexamined life is not worth living'. The answers are not as important as the process of examining. This cannot be done in a boisterous party but in solitude. Enjoy the parties and have a good time, do well at your job and rise up, but take a retreat occasionally, delve into an interpretation of what you are becoming or have become and at what cost.

In the world of ethics, you are all alone. Enjoy the solitude. Like Yudhishtira, in the end, the last walk is to be taken alone. He was accompanied till the door of heaven not by his brothers or wife, but by a dog. That dog was dharma.

CONCLUSION

So what should I say at the end of the book? What guidelines has the book given you? What is its conclusion?

As I had mentioned at the beginning, it does not *seek* to give you any clear-cut guidelines. Such guidelines cannot be given. As for the conclusion, it is that, in ethical matters, there is no conclusion. There are many conclusions, but only one of them is *your* conclusion, and you need to find that solution yourself.

Like in life itself, you have to decide whether you wish to be an ethical manager or not, and if yes, to what extent. That decision is yours, and yours alone. This book cannot tell you what kind of a manager you should become. But if you think there is something to say for being an ethical manager, hopefully the book has given some guidelines.

KEY TAKEAWAYS

1. There is no one you need to be answerable to on ethical matters—except yourself.

2. Ethics cannot be pursued for the reason that it pays. You follow it because you feel it is the right way. If you do not feel that way, dump ethics.

3. There is no such thing as *the* right thing to do in every circumstance. There are no rules or theories to tell you

what is right; theories may guide you, but the decision is yours, and yours alone.

REFERENCES

Golding, W. 1954. *The Lord of the Flies*. London: Faber & Faber.
Manikutty, S., Forthcoming. 'Why Should I be Ethical? Some Answers from Mahabharatha', *Journal of Human Values*.

Acknowledgements

I wish to thank the numerous students I have taught in the PGP, PGPX, and PGP PMP in the subjects of leadership and ethics whose insights have enriched this book. This book could not have been the same without their contributions to class discussions, term papers, and those (perhaps hated at that time) 9.15 pm pre-class discussions.

I wish to thank the IIMA and its director, Professor Samir Barua, and Professor Jayant Varma for this initiative of bringing out this book as a part of the IIMA Random House Books series on different topics.

Thanks are due to the editors at Random House India, Chiki Sarkar, Priyanka Sarkar, and Milee Ashwarya for their support, and the anonymous copy editor who did a great job of editing the manuscript.

I wish to place on record my appreciation for the excellent typing of the manuscript done by my secretary, Ramany Vijayapalan.

A note on IIMA Business Books

The IIM Ahmedabad Business Books bring key issues in management and business to a general audience. With a wealth of information and illustrations from contemporary Indian businesses, these non-academic and user-friendly books from the faculty of IIM Ahmedabad are essential corporate reading. www.iimabooks.com

Would you like to participate

in the IIMA Guru Yatra?

For more details visit

www.iimabooks.com

OTHER BOOKS IN THIS SERIES

THE PERSUASIVE MANAGER
Communication Strategies for 21st Century Managers
M.M. MONIPPALLY

STRATEGIES FOR GROWTH
Help Your Business Move Up the Ladder
ATANU GHOSH

BUSINESS AND INTELLECTUAL PROPERTY
Protect Your Idea
ANURAG K. AGARWAL

MANAGERS WHO MAKE A DIFFERENCE
Sharpening Your Management Skills
T.V. RAO

LEADING FROM THE TOP
Directors Who Make the Difference
N. BALASUBRAMANIAN

SPEAK WITH IMPACT
MEENAKSHI SHARMA

WHY I AM PAYING MORE
Price Theory and Market Structures Made Simple
SATISH Y. DEODHAR

MYSTERIES IN MANAGEMENT
AJEET N. MATHUR

HOW TO MAKE THE RIGHT DECISION
ARNAB K. LAHA